MILESTONES

A Word of Faith,

Holy Spirit Empowered

Addiction Recovery Guide

An Interactive Workbook to

Take You on a Venture of

Discovering Who You Are in Christ

by Cynthia Major Almaraz

Harrison House
Tulsa, OK

TABLE OF CONTENTS

DEDICATIONS

This book is dedicated to my spiritual parents and family ...

To B.B. & Velma Hankins, (who have since graduated to heaven), without them I would not be here today. They were not afraid to get too close to the girl from jail! Their unconditional love and that of their church, West Columbia Christian Center of Texas, showed me true Christianity.

To my wonderful husband, Robert John Almaraz, your support, patience and above all, pure heart towards God continue to encourage me day by day. You are the love of my life.

To Dale, my first born, you are my soldier son, the one who has endured many hardships, but you are like a rock that is steady and immovable. Your determination and "never give up" attitude have made you who you are today! I am so proud of you and your love for the Lord, your country, and family. May your latter years be your best years!

To Will, my miracle son, when I was told I could not have any more children – you came, and what an adventure it has been watching you grow up! The first day, you were winning everyone with your charm and excitement to see the world. And that you continue to do with your endless passion for missions and true heartfelt worship. Your heart is that of David, as was prophesied over you many times. You have allowed music to heal your soul and you share that in all your Holy Spirit inspired songs. May you continue to create an environment of worship and lead others into His holy presence.

To Stephen, my third and last son, you are another miracle baby. You are my quiet son - the thinker and a music prodigy! May you use all your God- given talents for the kingdom as was prophesied over you as well – for it is said you are a master builder in the house of God. I look forward to what is ahead as you put the Lord first. All your dreams will come true!

To my Savior and Lord Jesus Christ, thank you for setting me free from a nightmare life of darkness and despair. I was truly lost and stuck and only You could save me and pull me up out of the hopelessness that engulfed me. You are the one who has stabilized me and given me a hope and a future. I am eternally grateful and will tell my story-Your story to all who will listen.

FOREWORD

Can anything good come out of West Columbia, Texas?
The answer is a resounding YES!
Cindy Almaraz is living proof!

Vicki and I met Cindy in the Fall of 1977 at THE CHRISTIAN CENTER in West Columbia. We were serving there with my Pastors and parents, B. B. & Velma Hankins.

Cindy met Jesus and was gloriously born again and set free in the BRAZORIA COUNTY JAIL in Angleton, Texas in October of that year! Cindy's encounter was a result of THE CHRISTIAN CENTER'S County Jail Ministry Team who held a Sunday afternoon service every week! At that time it was the only jail ministry allowed in the county jail, and they never missed a Sunday regardless of weather, holidays, or personal situations! My father was a faithful man of God who believed and exampled the same in his life! As a result the County Jail services were always conducted. Often I've wondered what would've happened if they had decided not to go the Sunday that Cindy met the Lord?

Subsequently, it has been a delight for Vicki and me to know Cindy for almost 40 years. During her time at the church, we saw God begin to restore her life. Cindy's early release from jail was a miracle in itself! A real "God-event"! Next, the Lord restored her son, Dale, back to her after losing custody of him due to her previous lifestyle that had resulted in her incarceration!

Cindy's walk with Christ began in the church in West Columbia. The church sent her then to further her discipleship at CFNI in

Dallas, and eventually to RHEMA BIBLE TRAINING CENTER in Tulsa.

Cindy's story is an illustration of how an encounter with Jesus can change one's life! Some people do whatever they can. Cindy did whatever it took!

Knowing that God is no respecter of persons, I am convinced that anyone reading this book will be challenged, changed, and blessed!

MICHAEL HANKINS , PASTOR OF CHURCH IN THE CITY, ROWLETT, TX

INTRODUCTION

This book was written to provide a faith-based addiction recovery guide that emphasizes the power of the spoken Word of God combined with the empowerment of the Holy Spirit. I believe these two elements are vital in maintaining sobriety in addiction recovery. This book is an accumulation of things that I have learned and applied in my own life over the past thirty-seven years. I have seen many lives transformed by using the principles outlined in this book. People have moved out from their past and into their God-given future. The only real cure for any kind of addiction—whether alcohol, drugs, pornography, food or co-dependency—is a personal relationship with Jesus Christ and receiving all He has through His Word and His Spirit.

To pursue recovery, it will take a sincere heart seeking true recovery with an attitude of "it is a life or death situation." Many do attend drug programs for not always the right reason. Some come to meet other drug connections, some to get their emotions comforted during times of crisis and then there are those who just want to fulfill court and family obligations. It will take the Holy Scriptures planted in one's heart, combined with the strength and power of the Holy Spirit; this is what will sustain a person through the storms and trials of life when they come. And believe me, they will come!

In ministering recovery, I believe we must focus most if not all of our energies on those who truly do want the help! Just like it says in the book of James, God resists the proud but gives grace to the humble. Much grace is available to the one who truly repents and wants to be free. People think they can sin all they want and they will be covered under grace. Don't be deceived! God is not mocked, for this grace is only available to the one who truly repents and allows God to transform his life.

We are not against physicians, counselors, rehabilitation centers, detoxification centers, AA, NA, CA, AL-ANON, CR, MM (Milestones Ministries) or any other program that has the common goal of helping those who are addicted to maintain true sobriety. Our desire is to bring together the natural and the supernatural to help people live their lives to the fullest! A lot of rehabilitation programs only bring an addict to the point where they get dried out and then realize that without divine intervention, it will be difficult to maintain their sobriety. Sheer willpower will only go so far, but with God's power— the sky's the limit!

We are convinced that if God is not in the picture, it is just a matter of time before relapse will occur. I guess one could stay in a program for fifteen years (I have seen some people do this) and attend meetings night after night to combat the fear of relapse. But this can become bondage in itself! Is that really the desired result – to live in fear the rest of one's life? Addictions already provided that! My husband was one of those who stayed in AA for eight years, religiously attending daily meetings. It helped him for a while but after receiving the Holy Spirit, he realized he needed more than what that program could offer. Most of all, he got delivered from the fear of relapse. He did so by spending his already limited time discovering who he was in Christ through the Word of God, instead of the Big Book.

God will help you come clean. As hard as coming clean can be, it really is the easiest part of recovery. The hardest part is maintaining your sobriety. That's where we come in with our Milestones program to get you rooted and settled in your faith so that you can maintain a life free from all addictions. Only God's Word can save your soul and change your desires. You must be changed from the inside out in order for lasting sobriety to take place. God always work from the inside out and not the outside in. He's the only "higher power" that can change you and sustain you! Then, your job is to maintain it by living your life completely devoted to Him.

The desired result in recovery is to live a life full of purpose and meaning without the fear of relapse ever again. God wants us to press on to our future, not stay stuck in the past. That's why we never say we are an alcoholic or an addict, because we know how vital words are. The heart is always revealed through a person's words! Instead, we confess what the Bible says about us: "We are brand new creatures in Christ, old things have passed away and all things have become new in our lives (2 Corinthians 5:17).

Are you ready to put the past in the past and press on to your future? If so, then this book is for you. I have been clean for thirty-seven years and my husband has been sober for more than twenty years. The principles shared in this book have sustained us. We are not just surviving, but we enjoy and live the good life in Christ by fulfilling our purpose now.

Milestones are not a one-time cure or quick fix, but rather a new way of living, a new way of thinking - a new life in Christ. So unless you are ready for a lifestyle change, this program can't help you. If you don't accept Jesus as your Lord and Savior, He cannot help you. Unless you admit you have a problem, no one can help you! There must first be the desire for change, then the dream of a better life. Then it takes making the decision to go in that direction. It starts with a step, an hour, a day and then it will become a milestone!

The Milestones came to me when I was reading the book of

Joshua, chapters 3-4. The children of Israel were finally being led into the promise land by their new leader Joshua. The Lord told them, "You have not been this way before! So set up twelve milestones in the midst of the Jordan River that was parted. It represents the journey and the crossing over that I've brought you through. This is to serve as a reminder of what I have done so that they may never forget it is I, the Lord who brought you out and brought you in. These are to be shared to all your generations." A milestone is a key event that is so significant that you never ever forget it, nor forget the Lord who brought you to it and through it.

Included in this book are stories of hope from those who attended our very first Milestone program (their names were changed to protect their privacy), and some excerpts from my own story, my husband Robert's, and my dear friend Patsy's story. Also included are important daily confessions, a few questionnaires, and of course the twelve milestones.

The Milestones curriculum can be customized to any church's recovery program. Since every church community has their own culture, our goal is not to come in and micro-manage the program but to provide the proven curriculum needed to get a program started to produce lasting results. However, if you do need assistance, Robert and I can come in as consultants for your recovery program or provide workshops to get it established. It is vital that churches have a recovery program. No longer can the Body of Christ – His Church- send people to the world for help! True, lasting recovery will only come through the Word of God, the power of the Holy Spirit and the genuine love of His people extending their hands.

THE SPIRIT OF ADDICTION – SOME OF MY STORY

I truly believe whatever happens to the physical part of a man first, happens to his spirit man. And I believe there are spirits of addiction. Why do you think liquor stores have signs that say: "Wine & Spirits"? Even the world acknowledges that drinking is associated with evil spirits. It opens the door for demons to come in and take control. That's why people say and do things when they are under the influence of drugs or alcohol that they would never do while sober.

I have visited countless inmates who have been incarcerated for crimes they could not recall. One lady passed out behind the wheel of her car and when she awoke, she was told she had killed a family of four. So for the next forty years, she was locked up and tormented with not even being able to remember the incident that put her in prison!

I recall as a child in my own household, observing my mother act like a puppet on a string, unable to control her own actions. She did things she could not remember and refused to believe them even if she could remember! I knew there was demoniac activity going on and I wasn't even a Christian at that time. There was this sense of darkness lurking over our family. I felt it had been there for previous generations, but I did not know how to explain these things.

I have learned, the word "drug" comes from the word "pharmacy." It is derived from the Greek word pharmakeia, which means medicine or drugs that inhibit a person's personality or change his behavior. These can also be called mind-altering drugs. In English, this refers to drugs given to provide temporary relief. This word is also associated with witchcraft, sorcery and magic. It more specifically means to be under the influence, particularly of evil spirits. Alcohol is a drug with the same kind of effects, which is why in the olden days, alcohol was used as medicine to numb pain during surgery or was given to someone who was very ill as they awaited death. In Proverbs 31:6, it says to give wine to those who are dying. When Jesus was hanging on the cross, a soldier tried to give Him such a mixture to help numb the suffering and pain. But Jesus refused it because He would not allow anything of this world to have control or influence over Him, even in His death.

The Bible tells us that spirits and alcohol go hand-in-hand. I personally believe any form of substance abuse has evil spirits attached to it and when one dabbles with booze or drugs, the demons are just waiting for that open door to come in and dominate that person's life. I have seen the same spirits of addiction move down from one generation to another, especially in my own family. I have family members who never drank, but when they took that first drink, they became a full-blown alcoholic! I know it was not just in the genes; there were spirits assigned to our family members, waiting for that open door to come in and to dominate.

My biological dad was consumed with gambling and alcohol. He died an early death at thirty-six years old when he was killed as a result of his addictions. This destroyed my mother. She was tormented for years, thinking maybe it was a "staged death" and he would come back to her eventually when it wasn't hot with the mob or the cops. Though I barely knew him, his life and death had a lasting impression on our family. Our family suffered tremendously over mom's "tears in the beer" lifestyle. She was trying to raise five children in a strange town without any form of income. We depended on her as our only caretaker, but instead, we were caring for her and running the household. We were children forced into adulthood too early!

I experienced demoniac activity firsthand as an addict. I was so desperate for a high. There was always this drive pushing me to get high. I remember a vision I once had after sniffing paint thinner (or whatever it was because I was so desperate for a high). In this vision, I saw myself living a lifestyle of prostitution and that it was my destiny that men would pass through me. I saw it so clearly. It was as though there was a movie screen right in front of me. But if I had followed that course for my life, I know I would not be here today to tell about it. Without God's divine intervention, it was just a matter of time before that vision became a reality in my life.

I ran away from home and joined a gang of misfits and from that moment, I lived in fear. I carried a brick in my shoulder bag, a switchblade in my boot, and I wore brass knuckles or big rings most of the time. When I was at home with my family and wasn't on one of my "runs" (I ran away thirteen times beginning at the age of 11 until I left home for good at 15), I couldn't wait for the man who brought my mom home from the bar to mess with me or to think he was going to take advantage of my mom. I had such anger that it was destructive to everyone in my path. I lived with a "payback" mentality toward all men. I guess this was deep rooted from never having a father who stuck around, and from witnessing all the pain my mother suffered just wanting to be loved by a man. She just kept picking the wrong man.

Thank God, someone was praying for me! I was on a suicide rampage—the ultimate goal of the enemy. I started envisioning my

funeral and staging my death. I was so tired of the drugs and felt
there was no way out. The thought of death started to appeal to me.
I found out years later that my mom's siblings in St. Louis, Missouri,
were interceding for all of us. I believe their prayers saved my life!

John 10:10 says the thief (Satan) is out to rob, to kill and destroy
us. I believe that drugs and alcohol are the biggest way the enemy
does this today. I have very few party buddies who are even alive and
if they are, they're either incarcerated or have become Christians, too.
Addiction is truly a life or death situation. We are playing Russian
roulette when we are trapped in addictions. Russian roulette is
when you put a gun to your head and pull the trigger over and over
until someone yells, "Roulette." There's only one bullet, so you have
a good chance of survival for a while, that is, until you keep pulling
that trigger. Eventually, it will be the loaded one you pull—then it's
goodbye to everything! This is the enemy's plan from the beginning,
to silence your witness for Christ. Addiction is like a game of roulette,
but addiction is not a game!

If mankind is set on destroying itself, then the devil has done
his job. This is a battle that is older than time, the battle between
Christ and the fallen angel, Lucifer. Satan is self-deceived, thinking
somehow he can defeat Christ, when Christ has already won the
battle. It is a done deal! It is over! Satan's days are numbered. So his
goal is to take out as many human beings (made in the image of God)
as he can as he is on his way to eternal agony and damnation. Why?
Because misery loves company and he is most miserable, knowing his
time is so short! Some say this sounds like a far-fetched movie, but it
is the Bible nevertheless. I've known demons, and now I know Christ.
There are certain spirits that I have been so familiar with that I can
see them instantly, such as lust and alcoholism. But it doesn't matter
what spirits I can see, it matters that Christ lives in me now. And

it is important that I share what He has done for me to save others from a life destined to hell and yes, even a life of hell on earth trapped in addictions!

When we dare to believe this truth that Christ has set us free and has redeemed us, then the devil can no longer destroy our lives. Our eyes become wide open as the truth of God's Word begins to flood our hearts with heaven's light. We can see clearly. We are no longer deceived. There is no more bondage when we can see what Christ has done for us and we humbly accept His restoration power. Then we can start speaking and using our authority when we submit ourselves to God, resist the devil and watch him flee in terror, as it says in James 4:7.

When you have a personal experience with Christ, you will know that you are loved and you have a Father who will never abandon you or let you go. When I realized that God would take care of me and protect me, I didn't have to run any more, I didn't have to fight anymore, I didn't have to be afraid any more, and I didn't have to try and kill myself anymore. His love truly did ransom me. He saves us from destruction. His love changes us from the inside out!

Since I received Christ as my Lord and Savior, my brother, one of my sisters, and my stepdad (while pretty much on his deathbed as a direct result of alcoholism), received Christ into their lives. My mom cries every time I mention Christ, but to this day, she is not sold out to Him. She grew up in a Pentecostal home, but eloped with my dad when she was eighteen. Then she was too ashamed to return home after my dad got arrested by the FBI. She did not want her family to say, "I told you so!" Unlike the prodigal son in Luke 15, she didn't go back home. Fear and shame have kept her away from home for all of these years. And now, most of her family are passed away.

I ran away from home as well, but to get saved! I hooked up with the same kind of people I was running away from and got busted. It landed me in a south Texas jail with felony drug charges. I have repeated some of the same mistakes as my mother. I have been separated from my family for almost four decades, never to live among them again. However, I did not stay away from them because of shame and guilt as my mom did; I stayed away to live for Christ.

In 1977, I bought a one- way plane ticket and ventured to a place I didn't know anything about—but God knew. I was searching for a new life and He found me, and I found Him. I loved my siblings and never planned to stay away from them. I just knew if I stayed in Pittsburgh, Pennsylvania, I would have died from either drug overdose or some gang related incident—being at the wrong place at the wrong time. I also wanted to spare my family from any negative consequences that could result from my wild lifestyle.

I have failed in several marriages, marrying co-dependents to take care of me and even an alcoholic, like Mom did. That shame and guilt killed any vision of ministry for me, so I thought. How could I tell anyone about the Lord with my life so marred? It was a lie from the enemy to silence me all these years. But now, I know better! I now share with all who will listen!

My mother has not yet returned to the Lord, though she grew up like her siblings hearing the Word of God. I have learned it takes more than just hearing and attending church. We must become doers of what we hear. Our Christian life really begins when we walk outside the church walls. How we live our lives and act outside of church is what matters and determines if we are really Christians or not. People are always watching to see if we have really changed.

Mom's oldest brother lived to be a ripe old age and never turned from God, two of her brothers were successful businessmen and also travelled, singing for the Lord. Her oldest sister attended Joyce Meyer's Bible study. Two other siblings chose to turn their backs on the Lord and went the way of addictions, which led to their early deaths. My maternal grandmother died at the age of fifty-five from heart failure, but was saved. My maternal grandfather died in his sins and addictions to tobacco and alcohol.

We don't realize how our lives affect so many other people, especially those in our families. That is why the Bible says that our life is not our own. Our choices in life have a direct affect on others, whether we want them to or not. They influence others and even many generations to come. We want the blessings to be passed down and not the generational curses!

After my transformation in Christ, my mother told me that her mom had prayed in tongues every night and even prayed for us before we were born. My grandmother frequented old time tent revivals with great men of God like Billy Graham and Oral Roberts. Her mother told her a lot about Christ, but not once did my mom ever tell me or my siblings about how we too could receive Christ and be saved. Some of my siblings have received the Lord through me.

I believe without Christ, we cannot survive any generational curse. But with Christ, our families can be saved. We can do something about our family's history. We can reverse the curses of addiction and sin that have dogged our families for so long.

My son who is now forty years old has never known his biological father, yet the same issues and addictions of his father have plagued his life as well. Why? I moved far away and I religiously taught him about the Lord, but to no avail. He had been in and out of prison. He was not truly grounded in Christ. I thought, "Where did I go wrong?" I cried endlessly to the Lord. Yet, I knew in my heart that I had opened the door many times with my "just a little rebellious and careless" attitude. I still had a wildness I didn't want tamed, even though I was now a Christian. I played with fire and not only did it burn me, but it burned my child as well. I compromised with the flesh and reaped its ugly consequences. Unfortunately, so did my child!

My son acknowledged Jesus as his Lord, but did he really know Him? He was saved at four years old and baptized in the Holy Ghost by the time he was six. He had experienced Jesus' love and forgiving power over and over again, seen miracles, yet had still opened the doors to addictions due to unresolved grief and bitterness. He also, like me and my father, experienced imprisonment. We all had a choice! But we chose destruction—saved or not saved. Why? Why does one get completely sold out and delivered and the other live a lukewarm existence? I can't take all the blame for my son because he is a grown man now and has a free will to choose God or not to choose Him. Today, he and his family do attend church and live a peaceful and quiet life. Dale is an honest, hardworking man, still proud of his Marine days and loves his country and mom very much. I love him. I do know we were just two kids growing up together and trying to survive in life.

> AS YOU CAN, SEE THE SINS OF FATHERS AND MOTHERS CAN AND DO AFFECT THEIR CHILDREN.

As you can, see the sins of fathers and mothers can and do affect their children. I know this firsthand. But I also know that just as quickly as they came, they can be stopped through the Word of God and by using our authority in Christ Jesus! We can shut the door to these addictions. I believe one of the reasons for this is because we stopped looking into the mirror of the Word of God (or perhaps we never knew who we were to begin with). We forgot. We forgot about our Heavenly Father. So instead, we go on our way like the fool in Proverbs 14:12, not knowing our way leads to death—to the death of our hopes and dreams, the death of God's vision, and the death of our ultimate purpose in life.

So why do we repeat the same "history" as our elders? Is it spiritual? Do familiar spirits stalk our families, waiting for us to open the wrong door? Does yielding to what seems like childhood fears such as snakes under our bed, spiders coming to get us, and the boogeymen in the closet, open the door to the wrong spirits? Somehow, I know they do if we don't know how to combat them by having Christ in our lives. These spirits of fear (fear of darkness, fear of abandonment, fear of strangers, fear of death, etc.) can grow into something far worse that leads people into more oppression and even possession and pushes them into making wrong choices. Silencing the torment by turning to alcohol, drugs or getting hooked on prescription medications seems to be prevalent today. Then if that isn't enough (which eventually it won't be), one ends up committing suicide to quiet the demons once and for all! But thank God that we have the knowledge of His love and the power through His Word - the authority to stop these demons and generational curse. However, we also have the same liberty and freedom of choice, to give up and give in and say, "I will go my own way; it's my choice- my life!"

There are so many things I am still trying to figure out, but these two things I do know: If we determine to pursue God with all of our hearts, we will live the life He intends for us to live. If we choose to live mediocre lives, we will never be satisfied and we will live in the torment of regret. Eventually, we will forget who we are and fall back into the same sins from which God brought us out. We will become worse than before, in fact the Bible says seven times worse (Matthew

12:45). We become like a dog returning to his vomit. (Proverbs 26:11). That's what a man is who looks into the mirror and then forgets what he looks like and who he is (James 1:23-24). He returns to his sins. So it is vital that we choose Christ so we can choose life.

If our self-talk doesn't change, if we can't see that we can change, then we won't change. We will never be able to change beyond our speaking and believing. I know that I am a new person in Christ Jesus. The old Cindy is dead and will never be resurrected again. She died when I received Christ in that jail cell one hot August day in 1977. I became alive in Christ to start living His purpose through me. I have not regretted one day, either! I am no longer in bondage; I am totally free. I don't need to get high ever again because He has filled that void in my life.

I am no longer tormented by demons as I once was growing up. I have peace now. Some say I have made peace with my demons. No, I have made peace with myself and most of all God! There's no more fighting and strife for me. I am now out to bless others, not to hurt and take from them as I once did. I am satisfied living the good life! I do believe my best days are ahead. My children are saved and love God. I am praying for the rest of my family to know Christ, and I believe they will! I have this hope founded on His promises that my household shall be saved.

THE RUNAWAY –
LISA'S STORY

Lisa ran away from home at thirty-nine years of age. She had
worked in the emergency center of her local New Jersey
hospital for over twenty years. As a nurse, she had always
cared for others—including her husband, two children and four
horses. She was the stabilizing force in her household. She said, "If I
fell apart, everyone fell apart!"

When she had a heart attack, she realized it was time to start
caring for herself if she wanted to live a long life. She had always
been a heavy smoker, a social drinker, and even an occasional
marijuana toker, but realized when the doctor said it was time to
quit, she just couldn't! It was now a matter of life or death for Lisa,
since she had a stint placed in her heart. She had to change her
destructive lifestyle, but she felt there was no encouragement from
her family to help her do this.

So one day, feeling like no one was there to care for her, she just
got in her big white Cadillac and disappeared! Eventually, she ended
up at her sister's house in Tulsa, Oklahoma. She was searching for
"real" answers such as her purpose for even being alive. She asked
herself over and over again, "What do I have to live for?"

She drove by a big mega church in Broken Arrow, Oklahoma,
and remembered seeing it on television. She had even watched some
of the services. She was so surprised how close it was to her sister's
house. Lisa had such a desire to visit this church, so the next Sunday

morning, she did just that! At the end of the service and with a tear-streaked face, Lisa made her way to the altar for prayer and gave her life to the Lord Jesus Christ that day.

The desire for alcohol and drugs instantly left her, but the desire for cigarettes didn't leave. Later she admitted that she didn't want to let go of the tobacco, because she liked her smokes! A month later, she attended our very first session of the church's addiction outreach program. She was the only one who attended that night, as my husband and I shared about the prodigal son who ran away from home. We had no idea Lisa had run away from home herself, but the Lord did—and He brought her to us! He directed her steps so she would come home to Him and know Him as her Father. That is how much He loves her. It was truly a divine set-up!

Lisa was so hungry to learn the Word of God. She always had so many questions and wanted homework and reading assignments. She needed more than just the rap circles or the once a week meeting. Since that time, Lisa has received the baptism of the Holy Spirit at our program. She also desired to attend Bible school, shocking everyone back home in Jersey! So the school put her on a probation period, since she was a new Christian. She started volunteering in many areas of the church as well. When she returned home for that summer, she and her husband had seemed to grow apart and she was concerned about their marriage. Affairs and drug abuse were also revealed. "It seemed I was so blinded to this before, but now through the help of the Holy Spirit, I could see clearly," she explained.

Lisa returned to attend her second year of college. Her grown kids were very happy for their mom's newfound freedom in Christ. However, they were not so sure it was for them so they kept their distance. That second summer she went home, she sold off some of her horses, settled family matters and returned with her now pregnant daughter, who had just graduated from high school. We didn't see her much that second year, due to her work schedule. She had to choose church or our program, so of course we encouraged her to go to church and get plugged in since she was doing so well in her recovery. As of this writing, she has decided to return back to New Jersey upon graduation. She says she will get planted in a church there with her husband and daughter.

"No more running," Lisa said. "It is time to go home and tell others about the Lord so they can have a better life as well, living addiction free, like me!" Lisa plans to start a community outreach program that includes a feeding ministry and a drug program and of course, use our Milestones. She says that she still deals with issues, such as the battle to smoke. But she now knows she is not condemned if she messes up. She reminds herself of our motto: When I mess up, I fess up and most of all, I get back up! She devours her Bible—day and night—and is excited about her new life in Christ. "You know, running away from home was the best thing that ever happened to me," she says. "It saved my life, and now my family! None of us will ever be the same!"

> "NO MORE RUNNING," LISA SAID. "IT IS TIME TO GO HOME AND TELL OTHERS ABOUT THE LORD SO THEY CAN HAVE A BETTER LIFE AS WELL, LIVING ADDICTION FREE, LIKE ME!"

Lisa is still learning to care of herself and prioritize life. While in school, she worked for a temp service to juggle her nursing jobs, college, prayer school, daughter and new grandbaby moved down with her during her second year of college.

She has grown by leaps and bounds, mainly because she has desired to change and then did something about it. She still works on co-dependent issues of wanting to fix everything and take care of everyone, but she is at rest, knowing her eternal destiny is secure. She no longer fears the future because she knows that God will take care of her and her future is in Him!

We had the opportunity to spend time with Lisa at her college banquet, during her first milestone of being sober in twenty years! She said it was important for us to be with her for this event. It was a new beginning for her. We are very thankful of how far she has come. She has a good life in Christ ahead of her and she is no longer tormented with fear. She realizes that it is okay to not feel guilty about taking care of herself first and start enjoying some of the good life that God meant for her all along. She can't wait to get back home and start riding her horses again. This is one of the things she said she is going to do for herself! (You go girl!)

TRAGEDY TO TRIUMPH: A LIFE WORTH LIVING — JUAN'S STORY

Our other son in the faith is twenty year old Juan. He came to us looking for a drug program since he was court-ordered to attend an addiction program due to his third count of possession of marijuana. He was ecstatic to find one like ours that was Word of Faith-based and used the Holy Scriptures as the answer to long term sobriety. He was serious about recovery and needed to get around those who were full of the Word and like-minded. In the past, he was never able to stay clean for court-ordered drug tests, so this was a milestone for him.

He came to us full of confidence and vitality, adding a breath of fresh air to our drug program. He seemed to always be in "high speed," transferring his old addictions for the things of the Lord. He was grateful to be alive and serving God, and soon we found out why. It took Juan a while to open up about personal issues, because all he wanted to talk about was the Word of God.

It is true that the old man is gone and all things have become new in our lives, but a lot of times one still has to seek professional help. Sitting in group sessions, talking things out that have been suppressed for many years is most helpful. If issues are not dealt with, they can really affect a person's self-worth and lead to ultimate destruction. Such was the case with Juan's mother and friend.

For some, a once- a-week drug recovery program is not going to be enough!

Juan grew up suffering much verbal and emotional abuse from his addicted mother who continually attempted suicide. Then she spent many years away from him in a psychiatric hospital. His father was rarely around. His grandmother raised him. He said, "The one who meant the most to me, my mom, never once told me I would amount to much in life. I needed her approval so badly!" However, he did have his praying grandmother and preacher uncle and aunt who loved him and encouraged him in the Lord. But he felt too guilty to be around them. He said, "I never realized that I didn't have to be a good enough person to follow and seek God, so I ran away from God and church, instead of to Him. I was so self-conscious, not Christ-conscious. I was focused on my sins and shortcomings instead of Christ's love for me."

> "THE ONE WHO MEANT THE MOST TO ME, MY MOM, NEVER ONCE TOLD ME I WOULD AMOUNT TO MUCH IN LIFE. I NEEDED HER APPROVAL SO BADLY!"

At the age of twelve, Juan returned home one night from a trip with his father and found a lot of cops at his house. They told him that his mother had shot herself in the heart and was dead in the bathroom. This added more fuel to his already negative self-worth. He took the blame as a young child, because he thought that somehow he could have stopped her because there were other attempted suicides that he rescued his mother from in the past.

Juan said he loved the Lord, but became disillusioned about Christianity after this happened and he moved in with his father. Now, he realizes it was just an excuse to not deal with his "stuffed anger." So instead, he outwardly lived recklessly on the edge, always experimenting with drugs and things he said he would never do. He said, "I just wanted to try what she had done (his mother), to get an understanding of why she acted and felt the way she did." He was searching for understanding about life in general.

He watched drugs destroy the ones nearest him and then he himself became addicted and it destroyed his athletic career. He was an MVP in every sport he ever played year round. "There was more than the drug addiction," he said. "I watched pornography, which led to sexual promiscuity in my high school years. In ninth grade when I showed up drunk at the school dance, I was kicked off the football team. Then I had to go to an alternative school. And just before my tenth grade year began, I was arrested with over two pounds of marijuana and spent a week in jail. I dropped out of tenth grade, but returned the second semester." He said he was just trying to silence the self-hatred that tormented him endlessly.

He rededicated his life to the Lord during that second semester and life couldn't have been better. Then summertime came and he began to slip as he hung out with his old friends again. Though Juan knew of God, He didn't know God in a close and intimate relationship. He was not baptized with the Holy Spirit until later on. He said, "I now know that had I been filled with the Holy Ghost with the evidence of speaking in tongues, I would have never gone on the downslide that I did from that point."

Juan also didn't understand about the authority that God had given him and that he could stop these thoughts from bombarding him by binding the enemy from his life and speaking to them. So instead, he tried to fight them off alone in his own strength, which is what he did most of the time by drowning the thoughts out by staying high.

Day by day, he drove under the influence, having close calls with the law. He lost his driver's license and barely graduated from school. His father was more of a friend than a dad, as he suffered from some of the same addictions, plus he had a gambling problem. They got evicted from two houses while Juan was in his junior and senior years of high school. It was a very unstable life. At his state wrestling championship, Juan and another player gathered money from the team to get some alcohol for after the tournament, but he and his friend ended up taking the fall for the team when the coach caught wind of it.

Juan then spent three months in alternative school. He knew he was digging himself into a deep hole from which he wouldn't be able to climb out, but he didn't know how to stop himself. "There were many days I would do a gas run and drive around smoking weed with a gun on my lap saying, 'I want to kill someone just to say that I have! Or maybe just kill myself!' I had absolutely no boundaries and was out of control." Juan wasn't thinking about his future; he was just thinking about the next high to help him cope with the next crisis.

One of his best friends from his middle school days invited him to live with him, so Juan moved back home and was near his relatives again. But one day, he came home to find his friend hanging by a noose in his front yard. He had killed himself as a solution to ending his drug problem. Juan was tormented with guilt that somehow he could have helped his friend and told him about God. So again, Juan reverted back to self-destruction. This recklessness led him to yet another arrest for felony possession of marijuana and more court order requirements to fulfill.

A year after this last incident, we met Juan. He was strong in the Lord, attending church and happy about living. He still had to fulfill the probation for the courts, but he was clean and passing all his drug tests. "Fifty- some drug tests," he exclaimed. "Three years of probation, 24 hours of DUI school, 24 hours of group counseling, six hours of single counseling, two A.A. classes per week, and a huge amount of money wasted," he said.

We were amazed how the courts gave him double credit to attend our church-based program. Our church has a lot of respect in the community and in the state of Oklahoma.

Juan now knows his Father God loves him and is excited about his future. "Even with all my setbacks, God was faithful to perform His Word when I called on Him to bring me up out of that horrible pit and well of intoxication." He has also been reacquainted with his biological father.

At this writing, Juan is on fire for the Lord and has completed one year of Bible college. He realized he had many teachers, but still needed a full-time "father" and was still having some of the same old struggles, so he has taken time off for accountability with an out-of-state pastor. His old friends were still hounding him, so we all felt it was necessary for him to relocate. The geographical cure of relocating doesn't work unless one has God in his life, then it can be the best thing that ever happens to that individual.

Juan faithfully attended our program for over a year and then became our assistant for another nine months. He always brought new folks to our program. No one could ever imagine that Juan had self-esteem issues because of his boldness for Christ. His life truly has been transformed and set free. Juan does have a life worth living now!

Juan says he realizes healing in the soul is a process and says he is walking it out day by day, one milestone at a time. Steps can be forgotten, but a milestone is never forgotten. Juan desires to be a missionary evangelist and has already travelled to many places and has witnessed firsthand the power of God in manifestation.

SWEET HOME ALABAMA – MARIE'S STORY

M arie was born into a family of five siblings in Alabama. Her dad was employed by a local factory for many years. Her mom was a CB club fanatic and talked to people all over the country on her radio. Their family seemed very stable, but then things changed and Marie didn't understand why. It was like they were trying to hide a family secret.

The family's first move occurred when Marie was four years old. The second move happened when she was five years old. The next when she was six years old. Then every year after that, it seemed like they moved and only stayed for her school year, and then they were back on the road again. Nothing was stable anymore!

She can remember being homeless when she was nine years old. Her whole family lived under a bridge for a while. Marie and her sister slept in the back of the pickup. The guys slept on the ground. Then her dad and older brother found shelter for the family at a dairy farm. The men agreed to work in exchange for rent. Her mom went off to another state to go to work or go to court—Marie wasn't sure.

Marie's mom returned in time for Christmas. She remembers receiving coloring books, crayons and a yarn doll made by her mom. "Mom was always leaving because she had to work. Sometimes the family was so hungry that Dad often hunted rabbits and squirrels in the nearby woods," said Marie. Her mom found work in Arkansas, so the whole family relocated again. Marie's older siblings seemed to be in trouble a lot with drugs and abusive relationships, so her mom was always bailing them out.

Then things got even harder in Arkansas. In 1982, work was scarce so the men walked from Arkansas to Dallas to find work. Once again, the family was on the move, this time to Dallas, Texas. By then, Marie was eleven years old and in the fifth grade. When they arrived in Dallas, they slept in the car and found a soup kitchen to eat at since they had no money yet. Her parents and oldest brother worked for temp services until they landed permanent jobs.

Things began to stabilize, but when Marie was in the seventh grade, her parents' health began to fail. The family returned to Alabama to be closer to her oldest sister. It was in Alabama that Marie met her true love, Richard. But it was also at this time that she was raped by her girlfriend's stepfather! When it seemed nothing was going to be done about the rape, her dad sent her away to relatives in another state where she started her tenth grade year. Richard moved with her. It didn't work out and soon the young couple headed back home to Alabama.

"MOM WAS ALWAYS LEAVING BECAUSE SHE HAD TO WORK. SOMETIMES THE FAMILY WAS SO HUNGRY THAT DAD OFTEN HUNTED RABBITS AND SQUIRRELS IN THE NEARBY WOODS,"

Marie dropped out of school in the tenth grade and married Richard. Soon she became pregnant and they moved into a trailer on Richard's family's land. Richard always worked hard to take care of Marie. Eventually, Marie's parents moved in with them and soon more family followed—four of her brother's children moved in with them when her brother was arrested for drugs. So guess who was taking care of everyone? Marie, of course!

Her parent's health was failing and the children needed better care since they had special needs. Marie also babysat her older sister's three children so she could finish up nursing school. Marie's parents were placed in a senior citizen's home. There, her mom was reminded of her once childhood relationship with Jesus. She rededicated her life to God and started attending church again through the nursing home ministry. It was at a tent meeting that Marie received Christ. A week later, Richard got saved!

Shortly after this, Daniel, another nephew, ended up on Marie's porch. He was delivered on her doorstep hours after birth and was placed into her arms. Months later, the state stepped in because of Daniel's mother's constant drug abuse. Marie and Richard were awarded custody of Daniel and his baby brother so the children wouldn't be separated from their family forever.

It seemed everyone was in crisis and Marie was always the caretaker. She lost her identity at such an early age because of all the responsibility others always dumped on her. She was violated and not protected as a young child. Her older siblings were high on drugs and she had to care for their children, as well as her parents—instead of being a child herself!

Marie harbored a lot of resentment. But after Jesus came into her life, she said her attitude changed. "One good thing that occurred through all of this, when the boys came to stay with us, "was that I had the privilege to hear each confess Jesus as their Lord and Savior. I believe that was why they all ended up in my care. The Lord had His hand on these little ones from the very beginning!"

Marie and her extended family moved to Oklahoma (yes, other

family members are still following her). Marie and Richard decided to attend Bible school. Things are much more stable now, although there are still some "real" family crises going on with the nephews' ongoing health issues. Two of the boys have severe disabilities. Marie says, "The Lord is my helper and I will not be afraid."

Marie volunteered at our drug program for almost three years. She first came so her nephew would go, since he was court-ordered (a perfect deed of a co-dependent.) Marie realized it was time to find herself again after all these years of suppressing pain, as well as her dreams and true desires. She has learned how to establish boundaries and not feel guilty if she says no to someone.

As a child growing up, Marie said she never had boundaries such as a bedtime, mealtime, or bath time. There was no structure because she never had much of a home life. She did whatever she wanted. She also said, "I never allowed anyone to get close to me except Richard and Jesus, and even that was limited. But now I am excited about being happy and finding out who I am in Christ." She is actually thinking she would like to go back to nursing school some day. She said it was something she wanted to do, but dropped out because of all the family needs. She felt like she had no choice but to put her desires on hold.

Marie says, "I am getting better and stronger in God. That's why the Lord sent me to the drug program, so I can learn how to overcome the past and be able to say hello to my future. I never drank or smoked or had any addiction issues, but I have dealt with these things with almost every family member. I've seen firsthand the effects of it with my nephews' health problems. So I am the co-dependent one, I guess you could say. I was still addicted, just addicted to a dysfunctional lifestyle of trying to fix others' problems that weren't mine to fix! I have carried unpacked junk for a long time.

This is my time to get healthy— emotionally and spiritually. I got a job, which means that others will have to carry some of the load around the house and help out. I am going to attend some prayer meetings and I going to be free to be me! I am learning and will know who I am. God will help me as I help myself."

Now, Richard and Marie both have graduated from Bible College and moved back to Marion, Alabama. Their family that followed them to Oklahoma have all returned to Alabama as well. There, they have land to live on that they inherited from their relatives. Richard is doing what he does best—fixing things! He's always been a great mechanic.

Marie had to quit working so she could continue caring for her elderly aunt, sister and special-needs sons. Now Marie has grandchildren that she takes care of as well! Today, she is an advocate even going as far as to Alabama's State Department of Education demanding that severely disabled children have equal rights and provision. They are paying attention to her! She is no longer quiet and pushed aside, but speaks out for justice and gives the Lord all the glory. She has the Word of God in her now to sustain her and knows how to pray for her loved ones, though it seems she is back to her codependent ways, she tells me. She says she does continually study the Milestones and Boundaries curriculum and is planning on teaching a program soon, if not to just help herself again! Her goal is to start a Christian bookstore and a drug program in her community. Marie wants to bring God's knowledge into their little town.

NOW I SEE THE LIGHT —
COLE'S STORY

Cole came from an immediate family of strong Christians. His mother, father and even his nine- year- old brother were filled with the Holy Spirit. But that wasn't the case with Cole. Even though he always sensed there was more, he never desired to pursue those things. At the age of thirteen, he became adventurous in a bad way. It started with a cigarette, then a beer, and then pot. He even fell away from playing basketball, which he loved. His grades plummeted. He went through all the usual stuff that accompanies drug usage.

Eventually Cole started using pills, then by the time he was sixteen years old, he was using cocaine. He got so bold that he even took drugs to school and started doing them in the bathroom. A lot of times, he would have his head down on his desk, pretending to be sleeping while chopping the drugs! Everyone seemed oblivious. That's when Cole's world really took a dive. He lost his car, his job, his grades, and the girl. Even with it all, he still kept going. He moved in with some friends to take the burden off of his family. He didn't see it then, but this was harder on them not knowing of his whereabouts or well-being.

Cole graduated a year later than planned, buying his way through night school. After school, he went to jail for distributing marijuana. Yet, he still kept going. He couldn't remember weeks at a time because of all the Xanax pills he had taken. Then he got arrested again, this time for DUI. God said that was enough! Somehow, Cole knew it was over and God changed his heart. Even though his flesh wanted to go back, he just couldn't. He knew it was over.

When Cole got out of jail, he was court-ordered to find an AA or any kind of addiction program. His wonderful mom found out about our church program and made him go to it. Cole said, "Which to this day, I believe is the only place that could have saved me. And the Lord knew I still wasn't willing and wanting, until a few weeks later when they got me filled with the Holy Spirit. It was God's time from then on! I was chatting up a storm like in the olden days before drugs. I was no longer shy or anything. I was truly a new person at that moment. I had full assurance that I was forgiven of my sins and now a new hope and a future awaited me."

Now Cole was able to hear the Lord's voice and felt like God wanted him to go to North Carolina for the summer. He said, "I like to think of it as basic training camp out there on the farm with my grandparents. God taught me so much out there. He got me away from everything for a while. I am so grateful that He was able to make it happen. I can see so clearly now!"

> "GOD TAUGHT ME SO MUCH OUT THERE. HE GOT ME AWAY FROM EVERYTHING FOR A WHILE. I AM SO GRATEFUL THAT HE WAS ABLE TO MAKE IT HAPPEN. I CAN SEE SO CLEARLY NOW!"

Cole's brother died from a skate board accident. Though Cole acted so strong at the funeral and gave an eloquent speech, he is still grieving tremendously over his brother's death and has regressed and pulled away from help. He avoids us, but is cordial if he sees us. He has married and parks cars for a living. I feel he has slid back into addictions and has hoodwinked his family into believing he is clean. But of course, time will reveal all. I hope not, but my gut and experience tell me otherwise.

Cole keeps his distance from us, which is another indicator to me. When someone is not doing well, they withdraw from the light and those who represent the light giver-Jesus. They can go through the motions and even attend church, but what is hidden will eventually come to light. He had a lot going for him, he graduated from our Bible college and got reunited with his uncle who is a well-known evangelist in England. He had an opportunity to work for him but declined and had regressed back into familiarity and his "safe zone" where no one gets too close. I care for him like my own son, but all I can do is pray from afar that he will come to his senses and come home like the prodigal son before it is too late.

A CLEAN HEART — PATSY'S STORY

Patsy was the youngest, born in a middle class family in a small southern Texas town. She had a mom, dad, two sisters and a brother. She grew up in the 60s and 70s and her parents loved her very much. She went to church when she was younger, but the only thing she got out of that particular denomination was a terrible fear that she was not going to make it to heaven, being told that there was no way of knowing for sure until after she died. At that point, of course, it would be too late to do anything about it! On top of that, Patsy had some really deep hurts that she did not know how to deal with and they haunted her.

Patsy said, "Ever since I can remember, I wanted to drink and smoke. By the time I was ten years old, I started drinking anything I could get my hands on. In high school, I turned to drugs as well. All I wanted to do was party. It seemed something was always missing in my life, it was as though there was a big hole in my heart. All I knew to do was to fill it with these things. I think I was trying to drown out all the fear and pain that I didn't know how to deal with otherwise. God would send people to speak into my life, to get me to turn the other way, but I would have nothing to do with it. I was so bitter. I even had a friend take me to a youth function when I was thirteen years old and I experienced the tangible presence of God for the first time, yet I still rejected it."

Patsy finally graduated from high school but still had no plan or purpose or even a good reason to be alive. She had so much fear that she wouldn't even go to bed by herself. She just drank or did drugs until she passed out on the living room floor or couch. She said, "I tried to always have a boyfriend around, not that I was in love, but just to have someone to keep me occupied so I didn't have to face my fears. Ultimately, I would drive them all away."

She said that she went on like this for years with things only getting worse. Along the way, she discovered crystal meth and loved it! She would go on several month binges doing meth, drinking, and partying. She even hung out with the big meth makers and dealers to make sure she had an abundant supply. There was a lot of money and nice things at first, but Satan never lets you stay in the good life for very long. He gets you hooked and then sets out to destroy you completely taking all you have, including those you care about the most and what little self- esteem you have left. Before it was all over with, Patsy was hanging out in crack houses and lost all of her friends and family.

Patsy said that a few years after she graduated, her parents rededicated their lives to God and began to pray in the family. But again, she resisted God. Eventually in 1986, she left the area and her parents didn't know where she was for three years until one day, she received a call from her ex-brother-in-law who happened to be a cop and managed to find her. He called to let her know that her brother had just committed suicide. Patsy was devastated! She loved her brother so much—and now he was gone! No goodbyes or closure! She said, "I had some contact with my family after that, but I mostly just sank deeper into drugs and alcohol."

A year later, Patsy got pregnant. She was twenty-nine years old and pregnant. She was faced with a major decision to continue like she was and lose her baby or really seek God and get free from her addictions and begin living her life with purpose. Finally, Patsy was faced with something bigger than she could handle on her own. She finally had something she wanted more than drugs. So she knew her only hope was in God.

Patsy began to read the Bible in search of answers. God started sending people into her life to pray with her. He showed her that He heard her and had not given up on her. Eventually, she was reunited with her family. They took her in so she could get back on her feet. She said, "I still was not totally surrendered to God, yet He ran to me first just like in the story of the prodigal son. He loved me anyways!"

She found Psalms 51:10 that says, "Create in me a clean heart, O God; and renew a right spirit within me." She asked God, "Could You do that for me?" She knew God was the answer because her heart was so hurt and hard from everything in her past. She had tried to get clean on her own, but was failing and now at five months pregnant, she still craved the drinking and drugging lifestyle. She knew she would die if her heart didn't change, but she felt so powerless on her own to change.

Patsy decided to go to church with her parents. During her first visit, she would not allow herself to surrender, even though she knew the Holy Spirit was tugging at her heart. The second time she went, she didn't even remember what the message was about but said, "I couldn't wait to get down the aisle when the pastor gave the salvation call." Instantly, Patsy was set free from all that had bound her for so long. She was amazed how God could heal her broken heart and make it clean again. Then He created in her a heart with new desires. She was set free from needing and wanting all the destructive things that had bound her for so long.

Twenty years later, Patsy is an ordained minister and happily married. She and her husband own and work a business together. Her daughter is married to a pastor and lives in Georgia.

"Has everything been a piece of cake? No!" But Patsy quickly adds, "I can't imagine living the last twenty years without God in it. Life is so much better when you can really live it and not just try to survive. God really does restore, heal and deliver! I will spend the rest of my life telling His story—and my story of what He has done for me!"

OPPOSITES ATTRACT — ELIZABETH AND CHARLES

Elizabeth grew up in a non-Christian home in England. Her mother started her in dance lessons at the age of two. By the time Liz was nine years old, she had performed with television stars, toured with a famous comedian and danced at the London Palladium (a theatre in London).

Elizabeth's home life had very little discipline and structure. Horror movies and pornography were frequently watched. This exposed her to much fear and sexual abuse by so-called family members and friends. Liz rarely attended school and when she did, it was because her brother, friends, family members or a taxi took her. By this time, her mom was ill with emphysema and her dad was dying of lung cancer. Meal times usually consisted of a taxi run to McDonalds, tinned food or food from a charity delivery service called Meals on Wheels.

When Liz was nine years old, her dad passed away. Then six months later, her mother also died. Liz became separated from her brother and was forced to live with her aunt. Before her mom's passing, she had made a promise to keep on dancing no matter what. To keep this promise, she delivered newspapers and also asked for dance lessons as her Christmas presents. Liz did quite well in keeping her promise in her dance lessons and public schooling. She made top grades in her classes.

However, life in her aunt's home was a different story. She was not able to see eye to eye with her aunt's alcoholic boyfriend, so a lot of verbal abuse came her way. Liz started to miss school and got involved with drugs. By the age of sixteen, she dropped out of school and moved away to another town to be closer to her brother.

A Christian lady named Vicky helped Liz with the move. She had first met Vicky at her brother's wedding when she was thirteen years old. At that time, Liz also first received Christ and became born again. Vicky would drive one hour one way just to pick up Liz and take her to church. Vicky did this for a while, but then it all stopped. Elizabeth felt alone again and didn't see much of her brother and his family as she so desired, mainly because because he bore a lot of guilt and shame and was dealing with his own past.

> "CREATE IN ME A CLEAN HEART, O GOD; AND RENEW A RIGHT SPIRIT WITHIN ME." SHE ASKED GOD, "COULD YOU DO THAT FOR ME?"

Elizabeth soon got involved with drugs such as cocaine, even while she lived in a youth hostel (halfway house) run by a Christian charity. While living there, Liz made connection with a man who had just gotten out of prison. He was the one who introduced her to heroin. Not long after that, she moved out of the house and began to live with the dealer so her drugs were free for the most part. The guy who initially introduced her to heroin knew men who would pay for sex. Her prison friend always took a cut of the money, too! He was not quite a pimp, just a drug addict looking for easy cash and she was the instrument he used to get it.

When Elizabeth's boyfriend decided he was finished with her, she was abandoned and left homeless, dumped on the streets. She began to cry, not for the loss of a home or a relationship, but wondering how she would pay for the next drug fix. She needed serious help so she went to the church where Vicky worked and met some people from Teen Challenge. She filled out an application to their program and got a reference from the pastor. Then she stayed with a preacher and his wife who had dealt with her issues before and could empathize with her.

After that, Liz moved out of town to get a fresh start. She moved in with an old family friend and previous dance teacher and his mother. But she says, "Even though the drugs were out of my system, they were not out of my head!" She dreamed about them and thought about them until eventually, she gave in to the urges and visited a drug counselor just to find contacts to dealers in the town. This is very common among drug users. People will think it is wonderful that abusers are attending a drug program for help when in reality, they are using it for drug connections. I have seen this happen over and over again.

At the age of seventeen, Liz was back on drugs. She witnessed someone overdose so she and another friend stole the dead guy's money to score crack before contacting the police. The next day, Liz was in complete shock of what had happened and was unable to stop herself from crying to the point she had a nervous breakdown. Once again, she made it to her counselor who was able to help her. She spent time in and out of a psychiatric ward after this occurrence. Liz was tormented endlessly with suicidal thoughts and voices because she felt she had let everyone down, including her mom. Since she couldn't see herself ever being free from the drugs, she chose to overdose. However, she failed and found herself connected to an ICU machine with a nurse by her side.

Three months later as she was recovering, Liz had hope instilled that her dancing career wasn't over yet, so she auditioned. She made a bargain with God, "If I get this opportunity, I will serve You the rest of my life!" Well, Elizabeth got the contract, but still did not serve God as promised. She continued smoking marijuana and drank heavily. By the time Liz was nineteen years old, she was still experimenting with drugs such as Ketamine and using cocaine regularly.

Eventually, out of desperation for a better life, Liz returned to her brother's town seeking love and acceptance. There she rededicated her life to Christ. It was in this town that she met Charles, her future husband. Charles grew up on the outskirts of England. His mum was a Christian and taught him to pray and read the Bible from an early age. They attended a Baptist church and he became a Christian around the age of seven. He had a stable family upbringing, which he enjoyed with his older brother Mick. At the age of eighteen, Charles moved to Scotland to train to be a dietitian and attended Brethren Church.

One night, Charles and his friend Adam were studying the book of Corinthians. They learned about the infilling of the Holy Spirit and speaking in tongues. Even though neither of them knew much about it, they wanted to have this experience for themselves so they prayed for each other. To their amazement and with little understanding, they were both filled with the Spirit like in the book of Acts chapter 2. This experience changed both of their lives forever!

After working as a dietitian in the hospital, Charles' work took him to another town, on the Northwest coast of England. He started to attend a church there that believed and taught on the things that he had started to experience. He was so excited about this! This is the church where he met Liz. He was so attracted to her. Her passion and zeal for life and her sense of adventure drew him to her. They began dating and got married two years later.

Liz still had a lot of abandonment issues from her past and when she and Charles argued, she would drink to try and escape the reality of the situation. Charles struggled to understand Elizabeth. Communication between them was poor during the first few years of their marriage. They moved to the United States in 2008 to attend Bible college for future ministerial training. This gave Liz the motivation to stop drinking and smoking since it was a requirement to attend the college. When she experienced the baptism of the Holy Spirit, she now had hope she could be successful because now she was relying on God's power and not her own.

Our addiction program helped Liz to understand some of her previous actions and to learn new coping strategies. It has also given Charles insight into his wife's addictive personality, as well as his own co-dependent ways. Our drug program has given them both the support they needed and has made them aware that these matters cannot be dealt with alone. They said the program has improved their marital relationship and has also showed them the importance of renewing their minds to the truth of the Word of God or nothing will change. They both say Milestones helped them to become the people God has called them to be.

> *"EVEN THOUGH THE DRUGS WERE OUT OF MY SYSTEM, THEY WERE NOT OUT OF MY HEAD!"*

At this writing, Elizabeth and Charles have graduated from college and return to their homeland of England. They volunteer in their church and help teach others how to overcome addictions and learn who they are in Christ. They have a beautiful three year old daughter now who sings and models, following in her mum's footsteps, but with Christ in her life.

We had the privilege of mentoring Liz and Charles for a while as spiritual parents and are so thankful for how far they have come. But we know for them to continue to be successful at whatever they do, they must stay plugged in at a healthy church of like-minded believers and immerse themselves in the Word of God. The addictive mindset doesn't change overnight! It will take constant self-examination and replacing one's thoughts with God's thoughts. And that is a life-long process, but a rewarding one!

"I DON'T WANT TO DIE!"— ROBERT'S STORY

Robert had been addicted to drugs for over twenty years. He first started smoking cigarettes in the seventh grade. This led to smoking pot. It was a way to cope because he was very hurt when he was eleven years old and his father left home, never to return. Robert lived with his mother and two brothers, one older and one younger, yet he still felt all alone. He felt like he was to blame somehow for his father leaving them and didn't know how to fix it.

The family lived in a poor part of Washington D.C. Robert said he always had to fight to show that he was not afraid of others. Otherwise, he would have been beaten up every day by the boys in the neighborhood. He became severely obese by the time he was thirteen for he used food as a source of comfort. But his obesity brought even more ridicule and harassment.

By the time Rob was sixteen years old, he lost a lot of the weight. Even though he looked good on the outside, he still felt extremely hopeless on the inside. He was so heavy into drinking, illicit sex and drugs that he didn't know how to get out.

After high school as he was trying to regain a relationship with his father, who now resided in Texas, Robert had an opportunity to be trained by his dad and helped run his diner. Robert loved cooking and seemed to have a knack for it like his father did. His father had served in the Air Force and was one of the personal chefs to President

Lyndon Johnson. However, Rob still felt an emptiness that his dad could not fill so after a few years, he returned back to D.C. and got a job as a chef in an upscale restaurant.

This new job posed other problems for Robert. He was now introduced to PCP and cocaine. He began to routinely smoke both of these drugs and it made him become very fearful. He didn't want people to know his life was out of control. He was able to hide it for a while but he could not stop and he wanted to get help somehow, but did not know what to do. He said after four years straight of smoking crack on a daily basis, he was ready for a change, so he surrendered by admitting himself to a rehab. In October of 1988, he vividly remembers this milestone in his life. "I could not go on anymore, I was tired of running, tired of hurting, tired of lying, tired of stealing and most of all, I didn't want to die!" Robert finally came to his end.

He said, "I was on that rehab bed thinking, "How did I get so low to this point in my life?" I could not figure it out." He met a guy named Bill there, who told him such a profound statement that he had never thought of and didn't know was possible: "If you ask God to help you, He will." He wondered why God would even care after all the things he's done wrong.

Robert thought Bill was a nice guy, but this was Bill's fifth time in rehab because he was addicted to heroin and didn't really want to be free. Rob was perplexed and did not understand how Bill could not see that he was going to die if he didn't stop using the drugs. That night when he got alone, Rob prayed on his bed for the very first time to God. He knew deep down in his heart that the truth was staring at him in the face. "Bill was going to die, because he did not want to quit the addictions. On the other hand, God knew I would listen," he said.

This was the beginning of Robert's journey to recovery, a life of freedom from hopelessness and fear. The next day, he awoke from his sleep different. The compulsion to use drugs was all gone. Something had happened to him. He felt so much peace, like he never had experienced before. He knew God was with him now and that evil presence had lifted from him.

Even after being set free from drugs and alcohol, Rob still had to learn how to live this new life called sober, so he started visiting Alcoholics Anonymous programs to learn how to do this. He attended these meetings for eight years, but always felt like something was missing in his life, he just wasn't sure what it was. He was fearful if he missed a meeting that he would mess up, so he religiously attended. He was even a guest speaker for A. A. many times.

Robert got married and the pressures of a family and the responsibilities associated with it became very difficult to deal with. He started to feel confused and afraid again. Things were getting worse after he found out about his wife's obsession with credit cards. He had two cars repossessed due to her overspending, but she told him that his vehicles were stolen. He was shocked to find out they were so deep in debt. After two years of sobriety, one night Rob had a bad fight with his wife and the anger was so overwhelming that he took off and got drunk. He ended up in a car accident, which could have been fatal, had he not heard a voice say, "Put on your seatbelt." He knew it was God speaking to him. Even though he had serious injuries, he would have died if he had not worn his seatbelt. And everyone knew he never wore his seatbelt!

This was it for Robert! He decided he could not allow people to push his buttons any more to cause him to react and go into a self-destruct mode. He told himself, "I don't want to die!" That night was a turning point and every time he was tempted to give in under pressure again after that, he would remember that night and say to himself, "No, I won't drink because I don't want to die!" Through God's help, will power, support groups and sponsors, he was able to maintain sobriety for five years. But he always felt he could slip any time with a nagging voice always whispering to him. He still took prescribed medications, so he honestly admits looking back, that he wasn't all the way clean!

He moved to Virginia to get a fresh start. God heard his heart cry. A group of people came to his job and left a tract about Christ behind in the bathroom. Rob found it; he took it home and read it and prayed the prayer in the little pamphlet. The greatest thing to ever take place in Rob's life occurred—he received Jesus Christ as his Lord and Savior. Not only was God with Him, but He knew somehow He now lived inside of him! He said he began to desire to preach God's Word after that. He didn't understand this desire and wondered what it all meant.

> "I COULD NOT GO ON ANYMORE, I WAS TIRED OF RUNNING, TIRED OF HURTING, TIRED OF LYING, TIRED OF STEALING AND MOST OF ALL, I DIDN'T WANT TO DIE!"

Robert, still a chef, took another job in a beautiful area called Chesapeake Bay. He and his family lived on the water. Fishing was a way for him to get alone and enjoy God's peace. The Lord was working and was about to do another work in Rob's life. He and his family joined a church in Cobb Creek, Virginia. There, he received the infilling of the Holy Ghost. He said up until that day, he was still cussing, smoking cigarettes and was still taking antidepressants. But when the Holy Ghost came on and in him, all that left him! Robert was never the same after that day. So now another milestone occurred in his life.

Today, twenty years later, Rob is happy and serving God. He is addiction and prescription free and is not in fear of relapse ever again. He says, "I am a new man, no longer tormented with fear or by demons. The voices are gone and I only hear God's voice now!" Rob is growing stronger day by day, plugged into his church and enjoying life. He is remarried, is a five-star chef, a minister and helps others get drug-free. He says, "Listen! What the Lord has done for me, He will and wants to do for you! So allow God in and He will do miracles in your life, too. All you have to do is ask God and He will help you. Tell Him that you don't want to die, but you want to live!"

MILESTONE #1 — WE OVERCOME BY THE BLOOD

The first milestone is to admit that I have no power of my own and that I need divine intervention. The only way I can overcome any addiction is by receiving and accepting Jesus Christ as the Lord of my life. I must acknowledge that I am out of control and have no boundaries. I am helpless without Christ in my life.

Are you ready to believe His blood was shed for you so you could be set free from all the oppression and addictions of the enemy? If so, then you have decided to take a stand and you are about to experience a new life full of peace and freedom. It all starts when you acknowledge Jesus as your Savior. Then you need to take a step further and give Him lordship over your life. If He is now in charge of your life, then things are going to turn around for you. So get ready for an amazing journey as you venture out—one day at a time, one milestone at a time!

A milestone is a key event that takes place in your life and affects your future; it sets a precedent for the rest of your life. It is so memorable that you will never ever forget it. It makes you who you are; it sets the course for your future. These memorials or markers on the road of your life remind you what you have accomplished and where you are going. Some examples of milestones are graduation, marriage, birth of a child, receiving salvation, and to some - the first day of being sober.

> Day #1. Today is the beginning of the rest of my life. I will not leave here like I came, in Jesus' name. I have made a decision to change and God is helping me, God's people are helping me and most of all I am helping myself! I have been set free and I intend to stay free. In Jesus' name, I have come to believe and receive all that God has for me. Amen.

Revelation 12:11 says, *"And they overcame him by the blood of the Lamb, and by the word of their testimony; and they loved not their lives unto the death."*

Overcome means: Vanquish, conquer

The blood of the Lamb is The blood of Jesus

The word of my testimony is My truth and honesty and faith

Nike is the Greek word that means Victory

The same word is used in Revelations 12:11 and in 1 John 5:4.

Jesus has done His part and now I have to do my part. It first starts with me daring to believe that God cares about me. He loves me and has a plan and purpose for my life. He wants me to stay free so I can fulfill my destiny. In Jesus' name, I am going to do just that. My future is bright in Christ. There is no more darkness for me, because I have been set free!

Jesus is the Son of God. He is God's Son. He became our substitute, the Sacrificial Lamb taking our sins upon His body and taking our place in hell so we would never have to experience it for ourselves. He now wants us to live a life of heaven on earth. Following Him is the least we can do for what He has done for us!

Say this: I am ready to start doing things God's way and not my way. God's Word is now going to become my manual for life. I want a new life and I know it all starts with me accepting Jesus as Lord and getting into the Word of God. As I look into the Holy Scriptures, I will find myself and what I have been looking for all my life.

Read Luke 15:11-32 in the KJV and Recovery Bible about the story of the prodigal son and his older brother.

The prodigal said to himself: _he deserved his living inheritance_

The older brother had what? _Served faithfully_

Did the father (who symbolizes God) show favoritism? _No_

Explain. _he let the prodigal son go find himself, having faith that he would find his way back to the fold,_

Will God do the same for you? _yes !!_ First John 5:4 says _for whatsoever is born of God overcometh the world and this is the victory that overcometh the world, even our faith_

Confession

I have come to the end of myself and have come to my senses. I am returning home to my Father God. I believe Jesus is the Son of God and I accept Him as my Lord and Savior. I may not understand everything right now, but I do know I need Christ in my life. I want to experience a life worth living. I want to fulfill my purpose and start being productive in life. Jesus says that He has come to give me life and to give it more abundantly.

I am tired of selfish living and feelings of no way out. I have tried everything else, forgive me, Lord. Now it is time to surrender to You once and for all. Please take me and make me Your child. Open my eyes to see and believe. Open my ears to hear Your voice loud and clear. Open my heart to receive and not forget Your Word. I confess You as my Lord and Savior this day, this hour—now. Please come into my life and totally set me free. I need Your help; I can't make it without You.

You said in Your Word that if I call upon You, You would take me up in Your arms and receive me. You said that You would never leave me and You would help me. Thank You. I believe You. I call upon You now, in Jesus' name, to do just that. Thank You that I am forgiven and my life is just now beginning. Hallelujah!

Today's Date: I received Christ or rededicated my life (today's date): _____

Day #2: I am a new person in Christ Jesus. Old things have passed away and all things have become new in my life. Read 2 Corinthians 5:17.

I am a new _____

The past is _____ and the future is _____ I have a second chance in life because of what Jesus has done for me. I am free!

Proverbs 16:25 says: _____

_____

My way is not the right way. I need God's way in my life. I

now want life, not death. I want to live and be all God meant for me to be, in Jesus' name. Amen.

Write down four things that you know are not right in the way you have been living:

_____

_____

_____

Confession

I thank You, Father God, for helping me in these areas and setting me free. I am a new creation in Christ Jesus now. And since I have repented, these areas are now a part of my past. I choose to press on to my future and let go of the past. I am forgiven of all my sins as I have asked forgiveness. So by faith, I ask in Jesus' name, Father God, forgive me and cleanse me from all sin in my life. I receive it by faith right now. Amen.

Take some time right now and ask your Heavenly Father to forgive you for whatever comes to your mind and then ask Him to completely set you free, once and for all. Be specific because He already knows it all anyway! Confess your sins and you will be cleansed and forgiven. First John 1:9 says, "If we confess our sins, he is faithful and just to forgive us our sins, and to cleanse us from all unrighteousness."

You may have to ask forgiveness in the beginning a lot, but don't be condemned for doing so. Just keep doing right and believing and receiving. Read Micah 6:8 and meditate on it.

Now write down four things that you know are the right way for you to live:

Romans 10:9-10 says: _____

_____

_____

I believe and I receive. Jesus is my Lord and Savior and I am His child—set free! Throughout the day, continue thanking your Father God for saving you and setting you free from all addictions and sin. If you prayed and gave your heart to Christ, your name is now written in the Lamb's Book of Life. You will never see hell's fire. You are a child of God with a good life to live and eternal life in heaven to look forward to after this earthly life.

Confession

This is the day the Lord has made, I will rejoice and be glad in it! Everything is turning around in my life. Good things are bound to happen to me now. I am excited about living again! God loves me. I love Him. I love myself now. I have a bright future and I will live it from this moment forward, in Jesus' name. Amen.

Day #3: Read and write out Ephesians 2:8-10 _____

_____

_____

_____

_____

_____

_____

_____

_____

_____

_____

_____

_____

_____

_____

_____

_____

Confession

I am saved through grace, not of myself. It is a gift from God. I acknowledge that my "works" can't ever get me into heaven. It is God's mercy that has saved me, and it's His blood and works that delivered me. He has created me for His works, so I am going to stop the bad works and start living His plan for my life.

I have a free will and I choose to live holy and right. I choose today to be free from addictions—drugs, alcohol and anything that would try to control me so I cannot exercise my free will. I choose to submit myself to my Lord and Savior Jesus Christ. I rebuke the devil from my life. I command you Satan, in Jesus' name, to leave me alone. Depart from me right now! Get out of my life, my house, my family and everything that belongs to me.

Write out Romans 5:17_____

_____

When we receive Jesus and make Him Lord over our lives, we reign over sin. Say: I thank You, Father, for making me a conqueror through Christ. Because He has defeated sin, I have defeated sin. As He is, so am I in this world. I am not afraid or rebellious anymore.

First John 4:4 says, "Ye are of God, little children, and have overcome them: because greater is he that is in you, than he that is in the world." I believe this and I receive it. Christ lives in me now. I am free, for whom the son of God sets free, is free indeed! Greater is He who lives in me than he who lives in the world.

What does "greater is He that is in you, than he that is in the world," mean to you?_____

_____

_____

_____

_____

Throughout the day, when thoughts of fear, cravings, or stress try to overwhelm you, say to yourself: I am strong in the Lord and in the power of His might; I do not rely on my own strength. Greater is He that is in me than the devil or any temptation that may come my way. I am free because the blood of Jesus Christ has made me free. I overcome by the blood of the Lamb and the word of my testimony. I live this day for the Lord. He is with me, He is for me, and now He lives in me! I am not alone. I will make it through to the other side. I cannot be defeated because I will not quit! Therefore, I win! Hallelujah!

Day #4: Galatians 2:20 says, "I am crucified with Christ: nevertheless I live; yet not I, but Christ liveth in me: and the life which I now live in the flesh I live by the faith of the Son of God, who loved me, and gave himself for me."

Confession

I know that Christ died for me so in turn, now I have died to my way of doing things. I have died to stubbornness, pride, selfishness, and sin—and I choose to live for Him. My old life, my old man, has been nailed to the cross with Christ. I am a new creation in Christ Jesus. The life that I live in the flesh, I live by the faith of the son of God who loves me and gave Himself for me. I give myself for Him.

Write down four things you can do or give to Christ: _____

_____

_____

Read and write out Philippians 4:13: _____

_____

_____

_____

I can do all things because Christ helps me. He lives in me and empowers me to overcome all sin. I know that addiction is sin. He gives me strength to overcome it. I take it one day at a time, in Jesus' name. Amen.

Psalms 23:1 says, "The Lord is _____; I shall not want."

Write down some things that you don't want anymore: _____

_____

_____

_____

_____

_____

The Lord is my shepherd. I do not want drugs. I do not want alcohol. I do not want cigarettes. I do not want pornography. I don't want anything in my life that enslaves me. I have been set free and delivered from all the powers of darkness, and I refuse to get pulled back into it. God strengthens me and enables me to stay free. I acknowledge that I can't do it without Him, but with Him—I can do all things. He lives in me, enabling me to stay free. The Son of God has set me free! Amen.

Begin to thank the Lord throughout the day for setting you free. Speak your thanks out loud so

you can hear it. Speak it out loud so the devil and his demons can hear it and flee! Speak it out loud so your old party buddies can hear it. Then they probably won't stick around either! Speak it so your family will hear it. But most of all, speak it so you will hear it. You are not ashamed to declare that your Heavenly Father has set you free. He pulled you out of the horrible pit of miry shame and firmly planted your feet on solid ground.

Confession is a vital part of your recovery. There are two kinds of confession: asking forgiveness and turning away from sin and "self-talk" confession.

In order for things to change in your life, you must repent. You must have a heart that wants to change. You also need to start talking about yourself and seeing yourself differently. As you do, you will begin to become transformed. Just as you used to live and breathe to get high, you must exchange your old high for the new high—Jesus Christ. Now you must live and breathe for Him. It's not your way anymore, but it's His way of doing things. You have to start thinking His thoughts now. Philippians 4:8 says, "Whatsoever things are true, whatsoever things are honest, whatsoever things are just, whatsoever things are pure, whatsoever things are lovely, whatsoever things are of good report; if there be any virtue, and if there be any praise, think on these things."

You will need to start listening to new thoughts, because as a man thinks in his heart, so is he (Proverbs 23:7). You are what you believe you are! That's why we do not say that we are alcoholics or addicts, instead we say that we have been set free and delivered. We put it in our past and do not keep it in our present so it doesn't become our future. For example, my husband Robert stayed in A.A. for eight years and realized he was not moving forward in life. He was still stuck confessing he was an alcoholic. He said he was going nowhere. Yet, he was so ready to make a change. We have to become so tired and disgusted about going nowhere that we are ready to do something about it. God is waiting on us to do just that! That's when He can help us. Your addictions must become a part of your past. You do not want to live in your past. You want to move on into the glorious future in Christ Jesus that awaits you. If I say that I am an alcoholic, I live in the present tense and I am still an alcoholic.

Day #5: Read Psalm 66:18. What does this Psalm say about sin or iniquity?

_____

_____

_____

The difference between sin and iniquity is that sin is missing the mark but iniquity is a stronghold of sins that have been reinforced by not confessing them and have been suppressed for many years. God wants you free from daily sin, but most of all, He wants you free from the sins that have bound you for so long that they have molded your life. He wants to do an overhaul in you, so to speak. Ask Him to do it and then allow it to take place and it will, day by day, as those layers are peeled back and removed. You will start experiencing a freedom you never knew existed. God wants you free!

Romans 6:23 says, "For the wages of sin is _____; but the gift of God is _____ _____."

In Romans 8:2 it says that Jesus has set me free from _____ _____ _____

If I mess up, what can I do to make it right? Write out 1 John 1:9 _____ _____ _____ _____ _____

Romans 8:1-2 tells me when I have sinned and repented there is _____ _____

Milestone Motto: If I mess up, I fess up and then I get up!

Romans 6: 10-14 and 8:13 says that sin can no longer reign in your body, but you have to take the first step and say no to it, then the Lord will empower you to stay strong and not even desire it. If you do your part, God is faithful to do His part. We have to do our part; we must work it daily by faith. That's what it means in the Bible when it says to work out your salvation. It takes WORK!

Read all of Romans 8 and slowly mediate upon these verses.

Write out one verse of your choice: _____

_____

_____

_____

_____

_____

Confession

I don't need to go around feeling condemned any longer, because I am God's child. I am forgiven. He loves me. He helps me to get back up when I fall down. I repent and that means that I do a complete turnaround in my life right now. I am not the person I used to be. I am a new creation in Christ Jesus. My life is new. I am sanctified and set apart to live for Christ now. The old man is dead and I am alive unto God forever!

> Day #6: John 10:10-11 says, "The thief cometh not, but for to steal, and to kill, and to destroy: I am come that they might have life, and that they might have it more abundantly. I am the good shepherd: the good shepherd gives his life for the sheep."

We are the sheep, Jesus is the Good Shepherd, and the thief is the devil— Satan. He is out to rob you, to wipe you out by destroying your health, your wealth, your family, and most of all, your life. But Jesus said He has come to give you life.

Abundance means a full and satisfying life. A life of addictions is a life of broken dreams, dissatisfaction, poor health, no wealth, no peace, and eventually an early death. The devil wants to steal your sanity. But Christ has given you a sound mind, full of peace and free from all fear. Isn't it clear? Anyone in their right mind would choose life!

Second Timothy 1:7 says, *"God has not given us the spirit of fear, but of power, and of love, and of a sound mind."* Therefore, I have a sound mind. I am not afraid. God has given me a spirit of love, of power and control over all the power of the enemy. I will not fear what the enemy can do unto me.

Read and memorize this scripture. It will comfort you in many situations to come.

Hebrews 13:5-6 tells us that the Lord is our helper. He is with me and will never, never, never leave me nor forsake me. He will not forsake me or abandon me. He is for me. He loves me. He lives in me. I am not comfortless; the Holy Spirit helps me and teaches me.

Write down four things God has done for you this week: _____

_____

Read all of Psalm 27 and say it out loud to yourself. Choose one of the verses to mediate on and write it out here._____

_____

_____

_____

_____

Confession

I hear my Father's voice and the voice of a stranger, I will not follow. He leads me and guides me by His Word and Spirit. God has not given me a spirit of fear, but of love, power and a sound mind. I am not alone, for He is always with me and is as close as the mention of His name—Jesus. I have been set free! I am redeemed! Amen.

Day #7: Read John 3:16-17. These verses talk about God's love for you. After you read this, write out what it means to you. God gave His all, so that you might have His all! _____

_____

_____

_____

_____

Write out your testimony of what God has done for you, how you made a decision to turn your life over to Jesus Christ, and what the Lord has delivered you from. _____

_____

_____

_____

_____

_____

_____

_____

_____

_____

_____

_____

_____

_____

Please complete this Milestone and bring it back next week to review in your group. Remember, anything in bold print is either a confession. Review this Milestone and confess it as many times as needed. Take your time. Go over it and make sure you look up the scriptures and meditate on them. You will do this every week.

This is how your life will change—one step at a time, one day at a time, one milestone at a time. A step is forgotten, but a milestone is never ever forgotten!

MILESTONE #2 — HOLY SPIRIT - DRUNK ON THE NEW WINE

The second milestone is to accept that I have no power of my own and I need divine intervention. I need supernatural help from on high to empower me. The only way I can truly overcome and resist temptation is through the help of God's Holy Spirit. I need to be filled and then continually drink from the living waters of God and get drunk on His new wine. I need to be strengthened on the inside with God's power.

I need the comforting peace of the Holy Spirit in my life. The Holy Spirit promises to be my helper and to teach me the right way to go and the bad way to shun. I need God's discernment and guidance in my life. I need boldness to say 'no' to unhealthy relationships and situations. I need to know how to pray when my head is giving me all sorts of problems. I need to be able to shut my mind off and pray in other tongues. The Word of God promises me guidance, strength, and wisdom through the Holy Spirit. I truly want to experience the high of the Most High and it will be the only high that I will ever need again, in Jesus' name!

Day #1: Today is the beginning of the rest of my life! I will not leave here like I came, in Jesus' name. I have made a decision to change. God will help me! I am not alone. God's people will help me. And most of all, I will help myself because I have been set free and I intend to stay free! Amen.

Ephesians 5:18 says, *"And be not drunk with wine, wherein is excess; but be filled with the Spirit."*

Drunk means: _____

_____

_____

To be drunk in the Holy Spirit means: _____

_____

_____

Isaiah 28 tells us that God is not pleased with His children drinking, and that the Holy Spirit is the only wine that they should be consuming, the new wine. In Isaiah, even the priests had defiled God's temple by getting drunk. Isaiah prophesied of the Holy Spirit in this chapter saying the Holy Spirit is the only intoxication that will ever provide God's people with a refreshing and true rest. He was so specific that he even described the tongues as stammering lips, though it was hundreds of years before the Holy Spirit ever came on the earth. Amazing!

God always provides a way of escape, a way out. The Holy Spirit is the only way to not give in to the flesh and lusts of this world. He is God's substitute for the real "get highs" of this world. When you are filled with the Spirit and continue to be filled as it says in Ephesians 5:18, you do not need anything else!

Why do people want to get high? _____

_____

_____

_____

_____

_____

_____

Mark 14:27-31, 66-72 says that Peter thinks he will be okay, but what did Jesus say he would do? _____

_____

_____

Peter was weak; he gave into the very thing he said he would never do. Has anyone else ever done that? Every one of us has to answer that in the affirmative, because we have all messed up and done things we regret! And afterwards, we felt ashamed, dirty, out of control, and most of all, powerless. We can all relate to Peter.

But God promises us all the power we need through the third person of the Trinity—the Holy Spirit. We need not ever feel hopeless or powerless again!

We may not understand everything about the Holy Spirit, but we must, by faith, believe and receive it just like we do everything else in our Christian walk. The more we grow in God, the more we will know the importance of the Holy Spirit in our lives.

In these last days, we need to stand strong and be able to hear God's voice. When so many other voices are speaking, we need to hear the Holy Spirit's voice loud and clear. Jesus said in John 16:7, "It is expedient for you that I go away: for if I go not away, the Comforter will not come unto you; but if I depart, I will send him unto you." Expedient means it is very important and of utmost urgency to act. Jesus knew the Holy Spirit, His Spirit, would be able to live inside of every Christian once He left the earth. This could not happen while He walked on the earth. We are living in the age of the dispensation of the Holy Spirit so it is vital for us to be hooked up to the Holy Spirit in these last hours when gross darkness covers the earth. As children of Light, we can shine brightly!

Peter failed because he had no power in himself to withstand the pressures around him. His heart's desire was to do the right thing, but he had no confidence in himself that he could be successful. He did what he said he wouldn't do because he was relying on his own understanding and human will power. If you rely on the flesh, you will fail; if you trust in God, you will overcome.

Something happened to Peter when he received the indwelling of the Holy Spirit. He wasn't like before; he became bold. He was no longer fearful or timid. He didn't fear the faces of the religious leaders or the heathen anymore. He was no longer afraid to rise up and say 'no' to sin. He could resist it and walk away. Peter became a great leader among his people. And he never again contemplated going back to his old job or lifestyle, once he got filled with the Holy Spirit!

Acts 1:8 says, "But ye shall receive power, after that the Holy Ghost is come upon you: and ye shall be witnesses unto me both in Jerusalem, and in all Judaea, and in Samaria, and unto the uttermost part of the earth." When you get filled with the Holy Spirit, you receive strength, boldness, and the ability to do things you couldn't do before. You will also receive boldness to be a witness. I'm sure you can testify of that if you are already Spirit-filled.

Some examples of Bible characters who did amazing feats when the Holy Spirit came upon them were Samson, Saul, Gideon, Elijah and David. But praise God, the Spirit just doesn't come upon us like in the Old Testament; the Holy Spirit comes to live on the inside of us. Peter, Paul, James, and all the other Apostles and the New Testament believers such as you and I have the Holy Spirit dwelling inside of us!

People get drunk in the world to have a good time or just to feel better. Some drink to reward themselves after working hard all week. They want to let it all hang out, so to speak, with no inhibition or fear. They want to forget about their troubles and cares, eat, drink and be merry. People say and do things when they are intoxicated that they would normally never do while sober. Then there are the nasty after-effects of drinking such as hugging the toilet, black-outs, breaking the law, harming one's body, harming others, damaged relationships, financial difficulties and many more regrets. The negative always outweighs the positive! However, the Holy Spirit will never make you regret anything. The world's way is destructive and it will cost you dearly. It is a counterfeit to the real thing. The Holy Spirit is the real deal!

According to Acts chapter 2, what happens to the disciples in the middle of the afternoon? _____

_____

_____

What did the people think they were doing? _____

_____

_____

The disciples were definitely not quiet anymore! They were not hiding like they did when Jesus was captured and crucified. They now had something to say, and they were bold. They were not afraid! The Holy Spirit chases out all fear. The Holy Spirit instills an overcomer mentality into the believer. You know the commercial that says, "Just say no to drugs"? Well, you can't say 'no' to them without the Holy Spirit's help! Read Acts 2:13-22, 2:38-41.

Write out what 1 John 4:4 says. _____

_____

_____

_____

_____

Confession

Dear Jesus, I believe You are the Son of God. I have accepted You into my heart and I want everything You have for me. I know the next step is being filled with Your Spirit and praying in tongues, so that is what I want. I am not afraid because I know all good things come from You. You wouldn't give me anything that is harmful. You said that all good things come from above, so I receive the gift of Your Holy Spirit right now. Right now, I am being filled with Your power, Your strength, Your wisdom, and Your peace.

From this moment forward, I make a quality decision to begin to pray in tongues every day. When I don't know what to pray or how to pray, I will pray in the Spirit. The devil doesn't know what I am saying, even my own mind doesn't know what I am saying. But I know it's my divine connection to You, my Heavenly Father.

Therefore, I will pray in the Spirit and I will walk in the Spirit. I will not fulfill the lust of the flesh anymore. This life that I now live in Christ is a supernatural life. I am not the old person I used to be, I am a new creation in Christ Jesus. Old things have passed away and all things have become new in my life. Today is a new day for me. I yield my life completely over to You. I'm so excited for what You have in store for my future! Amen.

Day #2: The Bible tells us that the Holy Spirit helps us in many ways. Jesus himself said in John 16:7 that it was important that He leave the earth so the Holy Spirit could come and live inside of every believer. While He was walking on the earth, Jesus could not be with every believer, but once He left not only could He be with every believer, but He could also dwell inside of every one of them through His Spirit. The devil thought he had it bad when one Jesus was on the earth, but now there are millions of little Christ's on the earth! Christian means "Christ-like one." Now we have God's power on the inside of us. I always tell everyone the Holy Spirit is our secret weapon that the world knows not of! But we do!

John 16 and Romans 8 in the Amplified version say that the Holy Spirit is all three persons in one. So I make these personal confessions in my life.

- The Holy Spirit is our comforter. He comforts me.

- The Holy Spirit is our helper. He helps me in all areas of my life. I am not alone.

- The Holy Spirit is our counselor. He counsels me to make right decisions.

- The Holy Spirit is our advocate. He protects me and defends me from all accusers.

- The Holy Spirit is our intercessor. He helps me pray when I don't know how to pray.

- The Holy Spirit is our strengthener. He infuses strength into me so I can stand strong.

- The Holy Spirit is our standby. He's my best friend, sticking by my side to advise me.

- The Holy Spirit instills confidence in us. I am bold as a lion and I can do all things.

- The Holy Spirit is our guide. He shows me the way to go, leading me on the right path.

- The Holy Spirit reveals things that are hidden. He shows me my future.

When we get saved, we receive some of these attributes to a degree. But when we get filled with the Holy Spirit, we can have all of these in their fullness. God gives us life and gives it to us more abundantly (John 10:10).

In Luke 11:9-13, it says if parents know how to give good gifts to their children, how much more does God by giving the Holy Spirit to them who ask. So ask! Then start activating the Holy Spirit within you by praying in tongues.

One way to live life to the fullest is by being full and continuing to stay filled. And as we learned in Ephesians 5:18, we are to be filled daily. The way we do this is by praying in tongues daily. Get started praying in your prayer language. You can start with five minutes a day and work your way up. Soon you will be singing in the Spirit, too. Songs will begin to pour out of you. You will do and say things you never thought you could do or say and be bold for Christ!

Confession

I love to pray in the Spirit. I am full of the Holy Spirit of God, and I have the mind of Christ. I am ever ready for every situation that comes my way. The Holy Spirit watches over me, anoints me, comforts me, enables me, strengthens me, and is always present with me. I am not alone. Jesus has done what He has promised; He has sent the Comforter to live on the inside of me. I am not alone; the Holy Spirit is with me until the very end.

Day #3: Read and write out Jude 20. _____

_____

_____

_____

_____

_____

We build ourselves up in God's language when we pray in tongues. When we pray in the Spirit, we reload our spirit or fill it up with God's Spirit. It's like filling your car up with gas when it is on empty. We get energized from the inside out when we pray in tongues. Romans 8:26-28 says when I don't know how to pray, I can pray in the Spirit. The Spirit knows the mind of God so I will pray according to His will and purposes, not mine. The Holy Spirit is the Great Intercessor and will pray through us using our tongues in intercession. Read and write out Romans 8:27. _____

_____

_____

_____

_____

_____

_____

First Corinthians 14:4 says, *"He that speaketh in an unknown tongue edifieth himself; but he that prophesieth edifieth the church."* Verse 14 says that my spirit is praying to God. Therefore, I want to pray in tongues often. Paul said in verses 17-18, when he prays in tongues, he gives thanks to God. He also says that he is thankful that he prays in tongues more than anyone he knows! In other words, he was praying every chance he could get. As you know, Paul did write the majority of the New Testament. I believe he got divine revelation from God through the Holy Spirit to write most of the New Testament. God is no respecter of persons; He will bless us as much as Paul. But the question is, How much are we willing to apply ourselves to praying in the Spirit to get answers and direction from the Lord?

Confession

When I pray in the Holy Spirit of God, my understanding does not know what I am praying because I am praying in another language, not the one I am used to speaking. My mind doesn't know what I am praying but neither does the enemy! The devil hates it when I pray in tongues. That's why I want to pray in the Spirit. If the enemy doesn't like it when I pray in the Spirit, I know I should be doing it for sure! I am as bold as a lion and I have the mind of Christ in me. I love my Father God and He abides in me. I am fulfilling the gospel of Christ as it says in Mark 16:15-18, "Go ye into all the world and preach the gospel to every creature. He that believeth and is baptized shall be saved; but he that believeth not shall be damned. And these signs shall follow them that believe; In my name shall they cast out devils; they shall speak with new tongues; they shall take up serpents; and if they drink any deadly thing, it shall not hurt them; they shall lay hands on the sick, and they shall recover." And that is what I will do, in Jesus' name. I will pray in the Spirit more than they all, because I want to be so full to overflowing that I get divine insight and revelation from the Lord.

Day #4: Read James 3:1-18. Write out the scripture that stands out to you. _____

_____

_____

_____

_____

_____

_____

_____

Bringing our tongue under the submission of the Holy Spirit is one of the most important things we must do in our Christian walk. The Bible says that it is impossible to tame the human tongue, and many have found that to be true! But with God's help, it is not impossible. Nothing is impossible with God on our side and living inside of us. We are not our own anymore. We have help—divine intervention! Through the Holy Spirit, we can tame our tongues.

I don't know about you, but that is one area that I have to work on every day! The Apostle Peter was another good example of someone who spoke before he thought. Some called him a "loose cannon," meaning that you never knew what he was going to say. And when he said something, it usually caused an explosive reaction! Things would be said at the most unexpected times. Without being controlled by the Spirit of God, we know our words can do a lot of damage, too. That is why it is so important to get control of our tongues and give them to the Lord. Praying in the Spirit will help you in the area of self-control. No man can tame the tongue, but God can!

Proverbs 18:21 says, "Death and life are in the power of the tongue: and they that love it shall eat the fruit thereof." You have the power and choice to speak words full of life or words full of death. Your own words can doom you! If you are always saying negative things, your heart will believe those words and guess what? You shall have them! Do you really want all the words you speak to come to pass? (Read Mark 11:23-24.)

It is so important to get filled and refilled with the Holy Spirit by praying in tongues daily. Peter could not stop cussing or get a grip on his emotions until he was baptized in the Holy Spirit. After he received the baptism of the Holy Spirit, fear left him and he became full of boldness. He also preached his first sermon and it was so convincing, 3,000 people got saved that day! Wow! Peter didn't run away or deny Christ any more after that either!

Confession

I will only allow the Word of God to come out of my mouth. I pray in tongues more than anything. My words minister life, not death. I am kind and tender-hearted. The law of kindness is on my lips. I will not grieve the Holy Spirit of God when I speak, that is why I pray in tongues and build up my inner man.

This is the day that the Lord has made and I will be glad in it. No weapon formed against me will prosper, in Jesus' name, and every tongue that rises up against me will be proven to be in the wrong. This is the heritage of the servants of the Lord, of whom I am. I am in Christ. He is in me. I have been set free to worship the Lord. When I speak, I bring glory to His name. I pray this in Jesus' name. Amen.

> Day #5: As we pray in the Spirit, we will be guided by the Spirit. As we walk in the Spirit, we will talk in the Spirit, and live by the Holy Spirit leading us, instead of our own desires of the natural man telling us what to do. Write out Galatians 5:16. _____
>
> _____
>
> _____
>
> _____
>
> _____

When we were in the flesh, we did the works of the flesh. But now that we are in Christ Jesus and full of His Holy Ghost power, we can say 'no' and resist the works of the flesh. Write out what the works of the flesh are as found in Galatians 5:19-21. _____

_____

_____

_____

_____

_____

Read about Jesus being led away in the wilderness by the Holy Spirit in Matthew 4:1-11. Why did the devil flee from Jesus? What did He say and what must you say? _____

_____

_____

The Bible says that Jesus was tempted in areas like we are tempted. First Corinthians 10:12-13 tells us to take heed lest we fall. It also says that there is no temptation that is common to man, that God didn't provide us with a way of escape, a way out. If we are truly looking for a way out that is!

First John 2:16 says, "For all that is in the world, the lust of the flesh, and the lust of the eyes, and the pride of life, is not of the Father, but is of the world." These are basically the three temptations of mankind and what Jesus experienced when He was tempted by the devil in the wilderness.

- The lust of the eye deals with what we see and want: covetousness, greed, selfishness.

- The lust of the flesh is not just seeing it, but going a step further and doing it. This includes things like immorality, sexual sins, drunkenness, drugs, gluttony, and smoking.

- The pride of life, which was Satan's downfall, is not having a thankful heart, thinking you deserve more, thinking that you are better than others, thinking that you don't need God, and considering yourself self-sufficient.

Confession

I live my life under the influence of the Holy Spirit. I am anointed to do great works for the kingdom of God. I am strong and empowered by the Holy Spirit of God, and that is how I can say 'no' to addictions and all the lusts of the flesh. In my own strength, I can do nothing, but because Christ lives in me, I can do all things through Him. He gives me the strength and ability to say 'no' to sin and 'yes' to His ways. He gives me the Holy Spirit to dwell inside of me.

I live and move and have my being in the Spirit of God. I do not follow the dictates of the flesh anymore. My body and mind do not control me anymore. I continue to fill my soul with the Word of God and recharge my spirit with the Holy Spirit. His Spirit gives me life. I live the abundant life now, the way God had always planned for me to live. Amen.

> Day#6: The result of spiritual growth is fruit. The fruit of the Holy Spirit is found in Galatians 5:22-23. The Bible says that we are known by the fruit that we produce. If you want to know what a person is like, see what kind of fruit he bears. Write out the fruit of the Spirit. _____
>
> _____
>
> _____
>
> _____
>
> _____
>
> _____
>
> _____
>
> _____
>
> _____

Which fruit do you need help producing the most? _____

_____

Read Matthew 7:15-23. Why do you think that God compares

us to trees? _____

_____

_____

_____

_____

_____

_____

Write out verse 20. _____

_____

_____

_____

_____

Confession

Lord, I want to bear fruit that helps me to grow and that is pleasing to you. By faith, I confess that I am gentle, longsuffering, kind, patient, meek, loving and faithful, and have self-control. I keep my word. I am quick to repent; I am slow to get angry. I am quick to forgive. I bear much fruit—what is in me is what comes out of me. Jesus lives in me now. He shines through my life so others may see and know Him as I know Him. To God be all the glory in my life. Amen

Day #7: Write out Acts 10:38. _____

_____

_____

_____

_____

_____

_____

If God anointed Jesus, He will anoint you as well. In the Old Testament, only prophets, priests and kings could be anointed, but now God has given His Holy Spirit to us all and has made us to be partakers of His divine nature. We all get the Holy Spirit just for the asking. We ask for Him, we receive Him by faith, and then we start speaking in new tongues and doing anointed works.

In the New Testament in which we are living in today, we don't just have the Holy Spirit come upon us. The Holy Spirit comes to live within us. Just like when Jesus walked on the earth, the Holy Spirit came upon Him and then in Him. This is how He was able to defeat the devil. He became like we are (as a man), so we could become like He is (a child of God). He showed us how to live this life victoriously, one day at a time! Scan the book of Mark to write down a few miracles that Jesus did after He became anointed and filled with the Holy Spirit of God.

_____

_____

_____

_____

_____

_____

_____

_____

_____

_____

_____

Acts 2-3, read what happened to Peter after he became empowered from on high in the upper room. Before Peter was filled with the Spirit, his tongue was out of control and he was dominated by his flesh. He had some boldness to live for Christ, but nothing like we read about in Acts 3 after he received the infilling of the Holy Spirit and began to speak in tongues. He became bold and could resist sin after that. God also wants you to do mighty works with the empowerment of the Holy Spirit.

Let's live life beyond the limits, over and above, exceedingly abundantly in Christ Jesus. Just like when we partied in the world and went overboard, now it is time to be excited about our lives in Christ. In John chapter 16 and 17, we read about the work of the Holy Spirit, and Jesus praying for Himself, His disciples, and then all the believers. We must first build ourselves up in Christ and get strong. Then we can reach those who are closest to us—and ultimately the world!

Confession

The Holy Spirit shows me how to pray and who I should pray for. The Holy Spirit leads me into all truth and reveals the future of what is to come. I am not afraid. I am bold because I build myself up on my most holy faith. I pray in tongues and fill my mind with the Word of God. I repent and forgive daily. I am strong in the Lord. My Father

God loves me. I love Him. I will fulfill all that I am called to do, in Jesus' name. Amen.

NOTES

_____

_____

_____

_____

_____

_____

_____

_____

_____

_____

_____

_____

_____

_____

MILESTONE #3 — TWO SIDES OF DAILY MAINTENANCE

The third milestone is to accept that I need divine intervention in my daily life. I must be able to maintain sobriety and that will only come through God's help. Daily maintenance is what I am responsible for: repentance and forgiveness. I know I must put on an attitude of repentance and forgiveness. I do this by asking for it and receiving it. Then I am able to give it out to others. I can't do this on my own; I need God's help in this area. I know I can't have a "payback" mentality anymore. God wants me to show mercy as mercy has been shown to me. This is the only way I can be victorious.

I must first take care of my own heart before I can help anyone else or even try to forgive them. I must first take the beam out of my eye, before I can try to take the splinter out of my brother's eye (Matthew 7: 3). In other words, I must examine my own heart first with an attitude of repentance. I must continually humble myself and admit when I am wrong. I must choose to believe and receive God's forgiving power in my life. And most of all, I must believe He will forgive me when I ask for it. When I am whole and know that I am forgiven, it will be a lot easier for me to consider helping someone else. I cannot give what I don't have!

God said King David was a man after his own heart. Well, David messed up a lot, but the reason why he was a man after God's heart was because he was always quick to repent and make things right. He forgave others as he was forgiven. This is what daily maintenance is all about! When you forgive others, you are released so your Heavenly Father can forgive you (Matthew 6:14).

The Lord's Prayer (Matthew 6:9-14) says we are to daily forgive those who trespass or sin against us. That means it can happen to us every day! We all get mistreated sometimes or have opportunities to be offended. But when this happens, we can't fall into the enemy's trap and stay offended. We need to shake it off quickly! Daily maintenance involves maintaining a clean heart by putting on an attitude of forgiveness toward others. We must constantly confess our sins and be quick to forgive others who have wronged us. Even if they don't deserve forgiveness, we are not doing it for them, but for us. It has to become our way of life now. Say, This is who I am now. I can't afford to let my heart become hardened ever again, and I won't, in Jesus' name!

> Day #1: Today is the beginning of the rest of my life! I will not leave here like I came, in Jesus' name. I have made a decision to change and God is helping me. I am not alone. God's people are helping me. And most of all, I am helping myself! Why? Because I have been set free and I intend to stay free! Amen.

John 3:16-17 says that God so loved the world that He gave... and He forgave! The cross serves as a constant reminder of God's love and forgiveness. God gave His all when He gave His Son, Jesus, so we could have His all—a brand new life through Jesus Christ. This is known as the Great Exchange. He did not send His Son into the world to condemn it, but to save it. The enemy condemns, not God. God never says that you are not good enough or have no value. He made a plan to restore mankind back to Himself through His Son. This is how valuable we are to Him!

The question isn't how much God loves us, but rather how much do we love ourselves? Even if we don't love ourselves, it doesn't matter because God still loves us. He loved us so much that He died for us! He gave His life so we could have His life. He loved us when we were yet sinners and unloving, when we were still in our messes. He says to come to Him just as we are and He will clean us up. Don't try to clean yourself up first, it never works that way! Read Ephesians 2:1-9.

After using drugs and drinking, we can feel as if no one cares about us. Addictions can leave us feeling spiritually bankrupt, ashamed, guilt-ridden and useless. We can even become suicidal if we stay in this grief state for too long. So how can we love ourselves again? We can love ourselves because of what Christ has done for us, not what we have done. It is based on His work, not ours. He loves us and believes in us. He has given us a brand new start if we can dare believe that Jesus has taken away our sin and shame. That means we can start fresh now! We get to start over! He came to set us free from all of our past so we can have a future.

The New Leaf Syndrome never works without God's help. People try to turn over a new leaf by moving away to somewhere no one knows them. Yet, they don't realize that wherever they go, their problems go with them. Why? Because their problems are inside of them, and it is just a matter of time before they resurface. They need to get delivered from their problems once and for all in order to get totally set free! God works from the inside out, not the outside in. Don't go back nor look back. Instead reach forward to the new life that lies ahead in Christ Jesus.

Second Corinthians 5:17-21 says, I am a _____

_____ . Old things have _____

away and all things have become _____ in my

life. He who knew no _____ became sin for me

that I might become the _____ of God in

Christ Jesus.

In John 21:15-17, how many times did Jesus ask Peter if he

loved him? _____

Some people say that number represents all aspects of a man's
life: spirit, soul and body. I do believe God is concerned with every
area of our lives, but it is up to us to give it to Him. He wants us to
cast all our concerns over on Him because we were not meant to carry
that heavy burden (1 Peter 5:7-8).

First John 1:9 says that God is faithful and just and if I

_____ my sins, God will _____ me

of my sins. He will _____ me from all unrighteousness.

Forgiveness makes it possible to go forward. It is like a fresh cup
of water to the soul. When we receive forgiveness, it is like taking
a good bath. We feel clean all over. Just as God's Word says, He
cleanses us from all unrighteousness. He cleans us from this world's
filth and sin.

The Rearview Mirror Syndrome is when one can't successfully
drive forward because he keeps looking back in the rearview mirror.
A new driver is often guilty of this. It is the same when a person
keeps looking back at his past; he can't go forward in Christ when he
does this. This happens, there is going to be a head-on collision just

waiting to happen! Stop looking backwards and go forward towards your destiny!

The key to living a life free from the past is to live your life in the _____. Many people desire a fresh start. They dream of having a second chance. Well, in Christ, you can! In fact, you can have as many chances as you need until you get it right. God never gives up on us. It is we who turn away from God and quit. If you are always looking back, you won't be able to see clearly to go forward. You are destined for a head-on collision this way!

The Canadian Inuit's have sign posts or milestones called "Inukshuks." These are ancient Indian markers made out of rocks and shaped in the form of a man. They are usually so gigantic that they can be seen for miles. At one time, these milestones were vital for the Inuits in need of direction, shelter, safety and food, especially in bad weather. Most of the time, it meant a life or death situation to get to that next milestone. These markers were made in the image of a man and pointed the way to a place where one could get provisions. Well, Jesus is our Inukshuk! He was made in the form of man to show us the way so that we may live and not die. Hallelujah!

While walking from one milestone to another, God will give us grace to make it. Daily we must trust the love of God. We must trust that He cares about us enough that He has given us the victory over addictions. When you receive His forgiveness, it is like taking a stand against guilt. Guilt and shame can't control you anymore! You have been released; so you must release yourself. You must forgive yourself. The weight of fear "to use" has been taken away. You have been set free from that pressure. God has done His part, now you must do your part and dare to believe you are free, and receive it by faith.

Daily maintenance is up to you; it is your part. Forgiveness is a decision just like repentance is a decision. It is changing one's mind and taking it one day at a time. Yesterday is already the past, today is now, but the future is whatever you want it to be!

Confession

Today, I choose to live drug free and alcohol free. No longer will anything control me. I yield myself to the control of God's Holy Spirit and His way in my life. I don't want my way anymore, I choose God's ways. I ask You, Heavenly Father, to forgive me right now this day and I receive it. Yesterday is gone; it is my past. I will not keep looking back. I choose to press forward to what lies ahead in Christ Jesus.

I vow this day to do my part and to do daily maintenance, which means I am quick to repent when I mess up, and then I get up and walk on. I don't stay in the pit of self-pity. I shake off all the offenses by forgiving myself. I choose to forgive others who have let me down or don't believe in me anymore. My Father God believes in me. He cleanses me from all unrighteousness when I repent. So that is all that matters! I keep my heart right and I am quick to repent. I am quick to change my mind and my ways to live a better way now. I choose God's way, and lay down my own way. Amen.

Day #2: Lord, how many times do I repent? How many times do I forgive those who hurt me or offend me? Matthew 18:21- 35 says that Peter asked this question and what was Jesus' response? _____

_____

Why do you think He said this? _____

_____

_____

_____

Read Matthew 18:23-35 and write out what you personally
have learned from this story: _____

_____

_____

_____

_____

_____

_____

_____

_____

_____

Repentance means doing a 180-degree turnaround. You were
going one way, then you stopped in the middle of it and did
an about face. You decided to go a different way. You changed
your mind. Your soul told your body that this is what you will
do now.

What are the two sides to daily maintenance? _____

_____

_____

Write out 1 John 1:9. This is a great scripture written to the
believer's and taught by John to use. So memorize it, because

you will use it daily. _____

_____

_____

_____

Unforgiveness brings torment therefore we do not want to harbor unforgiveness. We must get rid of it immediately by acting on 1 John 1:9. We must show compassion and mercy as it has been shown to us. We may not be able to forgive in our own strength, but through Christ, we can do all things through Him, who strengthens us and helps us (Philippians 4:13).

Peter asked the Lord how many times he should forgive someone who does him wrong, "seven times seven?" Jesus replied, "No, seventy times seven." Well, that mean 490 times, and I believe that was for one day! In other words, Jesus was saying that it has to be a heart attitude now, a mindset of quickly forgiving those who do you wrong. Immediately get it out of you before it takes root in you. Get rid of the offense! We can still forgive and stay at a distance, but we must forgive. There are some people you must stay away from to protect and guard your heart so you won't get hurt again. Proverbs 4:23 tells us it is vital to guard our emotions, what goes into our soul realm, for it will influence all the other aspects of our lives.

We cannot afford to allow resentment to build up as strongholds in our minds. These strongholds can trigger us to relapse and give up if we do. That is why it is so important for us to guard our emotions. We must guard our soul realm— our thoughts, attitude and free will. We also need to be aware of triggers that can cause a person to relapse.

Alcoholics Anonymous uses the acronym H.A.L.T. to describe these triggers: hungry, angry, lonely and tired. It is during these times that you must stop; it is not the time to make a decision – ever. Because you will most likely make the wrong one! Always monitor yourself to see if one of these triggers is leading you down the wrong path. Ask the Lord to open your eyes so you can recognize it before it happens.

Confession

I forgive others as Christ has forgiven me. The love of God is shed in my heart by the Holy Spirit who lives in me. Jesus Christ shed His blood for me. He has forgiven me not just once, but forever, and as many times as I need. I am cleansed by the blood of Christ; I am washed in His blood. I am a new creature in Christ Jesus; my past is gone. I am now seated with Christ in heavenly places. Alcohol, drugs, and any kind of addiction do not control me anymore! I resist all unhealthy relationships and things, in Jesus' name. Amen

Day #3: Romans 8:1-2 says: The power of the life-giving spirit through Christ Jesus has set me from the power of sin that leads to death. God says that he does not _____ us! Therefore, we should not _____ourselves. Christ has set us free from the law of _____ and _____

Write out John 3:17: _____

_____

_____

_____

_____

_____

God doesn't condemn us, but sometimes we have a hard time forgiving ourselves. Read 1 John 3:19-24. Focus on verse 20, "For if our heart condemns us, God is greater than our heart, and knows all things." When we just can't forgive ourselves, we can turn to the Lord and say, "I know You forgive me, so by faith, I receive it. I choose to move on and not get stuck in this grief cycle. I choose to allow my latter days to be greater than my first. I choose to start enjoying life in my soul. I will not beat myself up over things that are already in the past and I cannot change them. I do have a choice over my future, and I choose to live. I choose life."

Read all of Deuteronomy 30 and John 10. What kind of life does God want you to have? ___ _____

_____

_____

_____

Day#4: Read Romans chapter 5 in the Recovery Bible. It talks about repeated forgiveness.

Write out Romans 5:5. _____

_____

_____

_____

_____

Read Ephesians 4:28-30 (Amplified translation) and focus on verse 29. Write out that verse. _____

_____

_____

_____

A lot of times, our mouths are the first thing to trip us up. Some people say that you are "hung by your tongue." The mouth is an unruly thing, and we can't tame it on our own. We need God's Word in our minds so it will come out of our mouths! Because we mess up with our mouths by saying the wrong things and it leads to sin!

For example, Peter cursed like the world when we he was in fear or got mad (Matthew 26:74). Read James 3, especially where it says, no man can tame the tongue! But praise God, for He can tame it and He lives in us! So there is hope for us. When we mess up, we have to be quick to repent and when others mess up, especially with their words, we must be quick to forgive them and just let it go.

I start forgiving certain people before I even get around them, because I know they are going to try and jerk my chain and cause me to sin. Some are so cynical that they will say the

wrong things just to get me to react, so I have to be ready. They laugh and mock God!

Some people just love it when Christians fall. Misery loves company and these kinds of people are very miserable. Get away from those who aren't celebrating your recovery with you. It is vital that you heed this! If they are not for you, they are not for you! There's an old saying, "Be around those who celebrate you, not tolerate you." You will know the difference, trust me!

Confession

God, help me to control my tongue. I know it is impossible without Your help. Today I ask that You put a watch over my lips,

quicken my spirit when I am ready to mess up so I can be on guard
and prevent it. I want to always be ready to repent and to forgive.
I know that You live in me and You said You would help me. Your
Word says even a fool is considered wise when he doesn't open his
mouth. Make me wise; help me to be a good listener and to learn to be
slow to speak. I don't want to trip on my lip anymore.

In Jesus' name, I refuse to allow any corrupt communication
to come out of my mouth. I will get away from those who trigger me
to sin. I am strong in You, Lord, and in the power of Your might. This
day I will praise You with my mouth and sing of Your wonderful love
and mercies towards me all the day long. Amen.

> Day#5: Mark 11:23-25 says, "For verily I say unto
> you, That whosoever shall say unto this mountain, Be
> thou removed, and be thou cast into the sea; and shall
> not doubt in his heart, but shall believe that those
> things which he saith shall come to pass; he shall have
> whatsoever he saith. Therefore I say unto you, What
> things soever ye desire, when ye pray, believe that ye
> receive them, and ye shall have them. And when ye
> stand praying, forgive, if ye have ought against any:
> that your Father also which is in heaven may forgive
> you your trespasses."

In the Recovery Bible, Ephesians 1:7-8 says that God is so rich
in His kindness towards us that He purchased our freedom through
the blood of His son and our sins are forgiven. He has showered His
kindness on us along with all wisdom and understanding.

Write out Ephesians 1:8:_____

_____

Words to Know

Forgiveness - an act of forgiving, give up resentment, excused, let it go and move on!

Offense - to attack, assault, or be displeased by the actions of another

Shortcomings - neglect and performance of duty / Romans 3:23 says we have all fallen short

Trespasses - to annoy another, offense done to another, crossing over boundary lines

Remission - means: to pardon, let go, pass over; Jesus was our Passover Lamb.

During the time of Moses, when the death angel passed over the houses that were marked with the blood of the lamb; these homes couldn't be touched because they were protected by God. The sins of those individuals in those homes were remitted. God has remitted our sins. We have been pardoned! Our sins have been released and are not being held against us! Hallelujah!

Confession

I am covered by the blood of the Lamb! I am protected from all evil and harm from the wicked one when I believe and trust in God. Therefore, no evil or weapon formed against me will harm me. God takes care of His kids. I am one of his children. He loves me and has marked me with His blood, the blood of His dear Son Jesus. I am forgiven of all my sins. He has shown His kindness and I do receive it.

I may have trespassed, but I am forgiven. I may have shortcomings, but God makes me strong where I am weak. God has remitted my sins and since He has forgiven me, I am not going to keep bringing them up to Him. I move on and let them all go. I let go of those who have offended me. I let go of my shortcomings by living one day at a time. I forgive others so that I may be forgiven. I forgive myself.

> Day #6: Prayer will release you from bitterness and resentment (Matthew 5:44). What do you need to do to those who curse you or hate you, or to those who despitefully use you and persecute you? _____
>
> _____
>
> _____
>
> _____

How did you, in times past, react to those who used you, cursed you or hated you? _____

_____

_____

_____

Why are you changed now? _____

_____

_____

God doesn't want you to be used, hurt or cursed, but sometimes these things happen. In fact, they probably occur on a daily basis for some of us. Life is always a trial and whether we are going to pass it or not is always the challenge. The thing is, if we don't pass it, we will always have another opportunity just around the corner to try again. Life is always about the tests. They don't end just because you get born again, but now you have a way to deal with them when they come your way.

Addictions stunt our growth emotionally and mentally so when we became sober, we still didn't know how to deal with certain issues. We may still find ourselves wanting to react in the same old manner as before. Until our minds are renewed, we can expect this to happen. That is why it is so important to renew our minds with the Word of God. Then we will be able to respond calmly. Remember, the flesh always wants to react, but the spirit responds. The Holy Spirit gives us self-control if we exercise it.

We have to stop ourselves immediately and say, "No, I will learn how to handle this situation God's way and make the right decisions. I will not just mouth off any old thing that comes to my mind. I will put on the mind of Christ and deal with it and pass this test, in Jesus' name!" You do not have to befriend people who treat you poorly. (That is yet another lesson, Milestone #11 - Friend or Foe). Some people think that just because we are Christians, we can be walked on. But this is not true! In fact, if we allow ourselves to be treated this way, it doesn't bring God any glory, but rather shame to you and God's Holy Name. This also, may be a good indicator that you are in need of some boundaries.

God expects us to have healthy boundaries and be able to say 'yes' or 'no,' in order to resist sin and take a stand against unhealthy situations and people. You have a right to disassociate with certain individuals who do not live for God, but you don't have the right to act unmannerly or rude toward them. This is not the love of God! Remember, He loves them as much as He loves you. It is not your duty to hook up with them to try to win them for the Lord. It never works this way because you will be the one who ends up a mess!

Read Colossians 3:12. It says, "Put on therefore, as the elect of God, holy and beloved, bowels of mercies, kindness, humbleness of mind, meekness, longsuffering." We have to put on and put off all the time. Some people say you are just acting or putting on. Well, if you have to start out that way, then just do it! Eventually, it will come natural for you because this is the real you. Christ lives in you now so you have His nature on the inside of you. You can't act out the old ways as you did before.

Confession

I don't react like the world reacts, instead I walk in love and forgiveness—one day at a time. I choose to put on Christ and put off the old man I used to be. I am a new person in Christ. I put on forgiveness and put off resentment. I put on mercy and put off bitterness and resentment. I put off a "payback" mentality and I put on the love of God. I make the right decisions and Christ gives me wisdom to do so and to know the difference. In Jesus' name I pray. Amen.

Day #7: Write out Psalms 119:165._____

_____

_____

_____

_____

_____

_____

_____

Peace is a weapon that keeps the storms on the outside from getting on the inside of you. The peace of God is the most wonderful revelation you can get, next to the love of God. The peace of God will preserve and keep you. It will guard your emotions and heart from getting hurt again. The peace of God will also guide you from bad situations and bad people. It becomes an empire in your heart, leading you along the way. Peace is the opposite of strife. If you have one then you don't have the other. Sometimes the best way to deal with an offense is by holding your peace or not saying anything at all. It will put the fire out as long as you don't add any fuel to the fire or words to its flame. Being quiet can be hard for some of us, but God will help us if we really desire change.

Love God's Word and start reading one chapter of Proverbs every day. Proverbs talks a lot about controlling the tongue and how to use good judgment in situations, which a lot of us lack because of our past drug abuse days. The Word of God will give us wisdom so we can learn how to live this new life in Christ. If we can change our talking, we will save ourselves from a lot of heartache and stumbling along the way!

Isaiah 26:3 says, "Thou wilt keep him in perfect peace, whose mind is stayed on thee: because he trusts in thee." The person who focuses on Christ will have perfect peace from the Lord. That's His promise in His Word.

Confession

Lord, I thank You that as I put Your Word in my heart, it will help me so that I won't sin against You. When I get angry, I will run to Your Word instead. If I can't say anything good, then I won't say anything at all. I refuse to allow corrupt communication to come out of my mouth. I choose to find scriptures and think and speak them only.

I want Your thoughts in my mind. For Your thoughts will lead me to true peace and soundness of mind. I keep my mind stayed on you and You give me perfect peace as I trust in you. I love and mediate on Your Words all the day long. They will sustain me. Great peace do I have because I love Your law, Your Word, and nothing will cause me to stumble or fall along the way this day, in Jesus' name. Amen.

NOTES

_____

_____

_____

_____

_____

_____

_____

_____

_____

_____

_____

_____

_____

_____

_____

_____

_____

_____ _____

_____

MILESTONE #4 — TRUST AND BE TRUSTED

The fourth milestone is to accept that I need divine intervention in the area of trusting God and others. I must learn to trust by faith. I must become like a little child—like Jesus said, to be able to trust my Heavenly Father, to trust that His Word is true, and to trust that He loves me. I must also learn to trust others and realize that not everyone is out to get me or see me fail.

I understand that it may take time for others to trust in me again. I must accept the fact that some may never trust me again. I will have to live with that and press forward. I cannot afford to get stuck in a cycle of grief just because someone doesn't believe in me anymore. I understand that trust is earned and it is a process that occurs over time. It will not happen overnight for me. It will take time for me to trust others and for others to trust me again, so I will take it one day at a time, since that is all I can do. God will see me through because He is my helper! Amen.

> Day #1: Today is the beginning of the rest of my life. I will not leave here like I came, in Jesus' name. I have made a decision to change and God will help me. I am not alone. God's people will help me. And most of all, I will help myself because I have been set free, and I intend to stay free!

Read Matthew 14:24-31 and John 24-28. The storms of affliction come to all of us. They are just a part of life. The Bible talks about Thomas and Peter. Both men knew Jesus, but they could not believe in what He said until a storm occurred that changed their lives dramatically and changed their minds forever.

Peter was a man who could believe God at His Word, but Thomas had to see to believe. He saw a lot! But we never hear of Thomas going far for the Lord. Did Thomas even believe? Was he one who knew of God, but didn't know Him personally? God reached out to both of these men according to their faith—what they believed.

A bad storm arose while the disciples were in a boat, attempting to cross over to the other side. That was when they saw Jesus in the midst of the storm walking on the water. Peter was the only one who yelled out to Jesus, "Tell me to come to You and I will." We know Jesus just said one word to him, "COME!" So Peter walked on the water towards Jesus! Why didn't the other disciples get out of the boat? Why was Peter the only one who got out of the boat? He seemed to be the only one who believed God at His Word and acted on it. He trusted God at His Word. Perhaps the others were immobilized with fear? Fear is the opposite of faith. When one is consumed with fear, he will be paralyzed from being able to do anything.

On the other hand, Thomas said that he must see things happen before he would believe. Was he even in the boat? The Bible says that all the disciples were there, so didn't Thomas see this great miracle also? I'm sure he saw many miracles, but he just couldn't trust and believe. There are many Christians in the midst of mighty moves of God, yet they seem unaffected by them. They are still living in their same stagnant state, caught up in unbelief and even sin. They seem oblivious to the things of God. Why?

Was Thomas so consumed by the earthly things around him?

What hindered his faith? What hinders your faith? Did too many people lie to you or let you down? Why can't you believe? The Lord understood Peter and Thomas and met each one of them according to his faith, and He will do the same for you. He will meet you at the point of your believing. But you must take the first step and dare to trust—even if it is a small baby step! This is what faith is. Until you can trust God, you won't ever be able to trust in yourself or others.

Thomas was able to believe when he saw Jesus after His resurrection. He saw and touched the holes in Jesus' hands and in His side. We know years later, Thomas grew in his faith and was responsible for spreading the gospel to India and the eastern known world at that time!

What was the miracle that Peter did? _____

_____

What one word did Jesus say to Peter, that He is still saying

to us? _____

_____

What did Jesus do so that Thomas could believe? _____

_____

_____

_____

One word from God can change your life forever, if you dare to believe it. Peter dared and it was enough to cause him to walk on the water and over that storm. The impossible became possible. God can do the same in your life if you desire it enough. Well, do you?

Definition of trust: _____

_____

_____

_____

Why don't people trust us? _____

_____

_____

_____

_____

_____

Trust is another word for_____. This is what pleases God! When we believe, we will _____. In any successful relationship, trust is a vital ingredient. It is the same with God. One must take time to get to know the Father through spending time with Him, engaging in intimate conversation and reading His Word. It is important to study who Jesus is, because Jesus said, "If you have seen Me, you have seen the Father." So get to know Him!

Proverbs 3:5-8 says, *"Trust in the Lord with all your heart and do not lean on your own understanding. In all your ways acknowledge Him, and He will make your paths straight. Do not be wise in your own eyes; Fear the Lord and turn away from evil. It will be healing to your body and refreshment to your bones"* (NASB).

- I must trust in the Lord; I must choose to believe God at His Word.

- I must not lean to my own understanding. I tell my mind to be quiet and I try a new way of doing things – not my thoughts, but God's thoughts!

- I must trust Him in all my ways, in every area of my life, including my secrets and things that I have kept hidden

- Acknowledging Him means putting Him first, doing what would please Him instead of what I always want.

- I refuse to be wise in my own eyes, for my ways have not been the right way. God has a better plan for me and I dare to believe that. It says in Jeremiah 29:11 that He has a future and purpose planned out for me.

- I choose to turn away from evil. Alcohol, drugs, gambling and pornography are all evil to me. They will only kill and destroy all that is precious to me. So I must flee from it, for it is sin! I must separate from it. Since God hates it; I hate it! I desire to be holy as He is holy. Ephesians 5:1 says, "Be ye therefore followers of God, as dear children." That is what I must do!

Confession

In Jesus' name, my soul is getting healed and I am getting stronger day by day. I am not the person I was yesterday. I am a new creation in Christ Jesus today; old things have passed away and all things are becoming new in my life. My life is being transformed from glory to glory. My future is before me and it is whatever I choose to make it. God has given me the freedom to choose my destiny. Therefore, I choose life and not death. I choose gladness and not sorrow. I choose victory and not defeat. I choose a sound mind and not confusion. I choose to trust God and not pull away in fear. I can do all these things through Christ who strengthens me and helps me.

Day #2: Today, I choose to trust God's ways instead of my ways. I ask You, Father, to help me this day. With

You living in me and being for me, I can make it today. I ask You, Holy Spirit, to replace my desires with things that are holy and good for me. You said You give me the desires of my heart, and I literally ask You to do just that. Thank You in advance for hearing my prayers and answering them. I love You, Lord, and I know You love me. I trust in You and not in my own understanding. Psalm 37:3-5 says, "Trust in the Lord, and do good; so shall thou dwell in the land, and verily thou shall be fed. Delight thyself also in the Lord: and He shall give thee the desires of your heart. Commit thy way unto the Lord; trust also in Him; and He shall bring it to pass."

Maybe it is hard to trust other people because you've been hurt so much in the past. Maybe it is hard to even trust in your own relatives. Or maybe it is hard to trust yourself again because you have messed up so much. But you can, and you must trust God! We have all been let down, left out, neglected, misunderstood, abused and used. Get over it! You have no choice! Don't let it destroy the rest of your life. Don't let it have power over your future.

You keep feeding these thoughts when you keep them ever present in your mind, instead of letting them go and putting them in your past. You give them authority over you when you nurse them and temporarily medicate them. So instead, starve them to death! Don't let them thoughts control you any longer. Don't let it continue to build a wall around you so you can't get out. Say, "In Jesus' name, I am going to break out with God's help." Remember last week's milestone—forgiveness is the key to letting go and moving forward. You can experience a new way of life now by forgiving yourself and others along the way, day by day, milestone by milestone.

If you don't make a quality decision to trust God, then you won't make it. You must make a conscious effort to stop listening to your thoughts and decide you want God's way. And His way begins with His Word. The only way you will get to know Him is by spending time with Him, praying and talking to Him about your cares, fears, worries, hopes, dreams, desires, and reading the Bible every day. You have to want it more than anything else! It has to become your new "high," so to speak, so you will do whatever it takes to get it and maintain it.

Many of us don't understand why loved ones won't give us another chance. Well, maybe they are tired of always being the giver. Maybe they are tired of trying to appease you so you won't get angry. Maybe they are tired of taking care of you, feeding you, catering to you to the point that they have neglected their own life ambitions. Maybe they are exhausted from carrying the pressures that was never meant for one person to bear alone.

It is time for you to get your mind off of yourself before you lose everything that is so dear to you! You must start taking life very seriously. Stop laughing it off or minimizing it. You must grow up and see it in the right perspective. For some of you, this is it and then you're out in the streets – no more home or family to go back to if things don't change. For others, this is a death or life situation! Read Deuteronomy 28:1-15 to find out what happens when you choose God's way. Write down four things God promises you._____

_____

_____

_____

_____

_____

Read and write out Hebrews 13:5-6. _____

_____

_____

_____

_____

_____

_____

_____

_____

_____

_____

_____

Memorize these verses and speak them over and over on a daily basis. God is for you and He is now in you. You can't run and hide because He is wherever you go. Besides, you don't want to run from Him anymore. You now desire to run to Him. He may be the only one who has not given up on you. So don't run from Him but to Him!

In the Garden of Eden, Adam was afraid and hid from God when he messed up. God already knew Adam had sinned, yet He still called for Adam to fellowship with Him. He wanted to restore him. God wants to restore you. If you mess up, get back up and run to your Father God. Allow Him to restore and make you whole. Be honest with Him and then be honest to the closest person to you, whether your spouse, parents or a trusted friend.

By confiding in someone else about your weaknesses, you are saying, "I am exposing my sins, opening up my heart to get help." This will be the quickest way to gain trust again. When your loved ones see how sincere you are when you humble yourself, they will go out of their way to help you and will start to believe in you again.

Of course, it may take some time if you've done this repeatedly. If you have repented over and over again and haven't really changed, others may stay at a distance for a while to see if you are for real. If you keep committing yourself to a rehab, but then quit in a week and say you're clean, they are not going to believe you. They are not that stupid! They know you are leaving because you can't handle the withdrawals, and most of all because you are not clean and don't want to stay clean. You want to get high again!

Remember the story about the boy who cried wolf over and over again? When a wolf really did come, no one believed his cries so he was devoured by the wolf. Don't be like the boy who cried wolf! You'll have to prove yourself again. It will not be a "quick-fix," but it needs to become your new way of life in Christ.

Confession

I trust in the Lord with all my heart. He leads me and guides me with His eye. He is always with me, He is for me and He lives in me. He said He would never, never, never leave me nor forsake me. He is my helper and my comforter. I am not alone! I live in the light as He is in the light, and the works of darkness no longer control me—I expose them! I have been set free! Whom Jesus sets free, is free indeed. I choose life and not death. I live my life to please God; this is my true desire now. I don't do my own thing anymore; I choose His way. His ways leads to a life worth living and that is what I want now. I am not like the boy who cried wolf. I am transformed, and my words and actions are true! Amen.

Day #3: The Lord is my shepherd, I shall not want. I do not want alcohol, drugs or anything   that would be harmful to my life. Psalm 23 says the Lord is my shepherd, so I do not want. He leads me. He guides me. I can trust Him to take care of me. I may not be able to trust myself, but I can trust God; He lives inside of me to take care of me. I hear His voice and the voice of a stranger, I will not follow.

Sheep trust the shepherd to feed them, give them shelter and lead them out of harm's way. They instinctively follow the shepherd, because day after day, the shepherd takes care of them. Maybe they have to be nudged at times with the staff, yet they learn to trust. We have to, in a sense, be like the sheep. Think about training a puppy. It takes work! Likewise, it takes work to hear God's voice and to trust in His care.

Let's take a look at the different kinds of shepherds in John chapter 10. There's one type of shepherd who really loves his sheep and wants to protect them at any cost. Then there is the hireling, who is hired and paid wages to watch the sheep. His heart is not really with the sheep, but for himself. When hard times come (and they will come), he will be the first to quickly abandon the sheep. Have you ever had friends like that? They are so buddy-buddy while you have something they want like cash or stash. But when that is all gone, they are gone too! It's sad to say, but there are many people like this. Yes, even in church! But does that mean you stop going to church? No! Of course not! As Charles Capps said, "Yes, it's true, there are fruits, nuts and flakes in the body of Christ, but that doesn't mean you throw out the cereal!" In other words, that doesn't mean you stop being a Christian!

We must guard our hearts and ask the Lord to show us who are His "true sheep" – the ones who really love Him and who will love us.

Ask your Father God to open your eyes to see clearly those who are His sheep and those who are in "sheep's clothing," the deceivers. Since we have been deceivers in times past ourselves, it is usually very easy for us to spot them! So, if you get an impression that someone is not right, you are probably right. Trust God's Spirit inside of you and your own intuition and conscience in this area.

Once there was a guy (very attractive and my type) at Bible school, who watched me whenever I worshipped the Lord. I could feel his eyes all over me and it really bothered me. I was new in the Lord and I guess I moved a little worldly. I asked the Lord to help me in that area so I wouldn't draw attention to myself, because I really liked to dance and jump up and down. One day, this guy finally came up to me and said, "I've been watching you and I like how you move." I was screaming, "Yuk" to myself. Well, I found out real quickly what his motives were when I asked the Lord to reveal them to me. I ended up moving to the other side of the auditorium to avoid him. Not too long after that, he found another girl who fell for his smooth-talking and soon they both ran away to "be together." I don't know if they ever returned to school or got married, but it was definitely lust that united them and took them out of the plan of God for their lives at that time.

I desired a godly man to be attracted to me and not the wrong kind. But this was an area I really needed to grow in because I used to just hook up with anyone who showed an interest in me. That was how low my self-esteem was. It was several years before I could even let a man get close to me and trust again. But that was okay because I needed to learn to trust God in that area as well. I knew I couldn't rush it or I would definitely mess up again. I learned that to be safe, it is best to do things in groups. This way, one does not set themselves up to fall by being alone with the opposite sex. Believe me, it is not worth the consequences!

When we get lonely, we tend to settle for less than God's best. Many people have done this in times of loneliness and have experienced much sorrow as a result. Wait for God's best; trust Him to bring the right one at the right time. It really is worth the wait!

Read Ephesians 1:18 and write out this scripture. This is a good one to pray so you won't be deceived, and you will be able to see clearly. Kenneth E. Hagin (Dad Hagin to me) said he prayed the Ephesians prayer every day of his life! _____

_____

_____

_____

_____

_____

Confession

I hear my Father God's voice and no other voice do I follow. I am not deceived. I cannot be led astray because I know His voice. He leads me and guides me down the right path for my life. He tells me who is safe for me to be around and who is not. I trust Him. I am daily learning to trust His voice in me through His Holy Spirit and His Word. The eyes of my understanding are enlightened so I can clearly see His will and path before me.

Day #4: As I grow strong in the Lord, the old ways and the devil's habits will just fall off. The things of this world seem so undesirable to me now. I set my affection on things above and not on things of this earth. My life is hid in Christ. I am not my own. I have been bought with a price, the blood of my Lord Jesus Christ.

People see a change in me. They see God at work in me. They are learning to trust me again. In Jesus' name, I will not let them down because I will not let my Father God down! He believes in me. He tells me I can make it. Therefore, contrary to what some may think about me, I can make it. I dare to believe that it is not too late for me to change.

God is my helper. I can do all things through Christ who strengthens me. I am a new person in Christ; old things have passed away and all things have become new in my life. God has given me a second chance! I will not fail in Him. Amen.

How can I get people to trust me again? Write out three things that you must do for people to believe you are a person of your word? _____

_____

_____

_____

Remember Psalm 37:3 says, to trust in the Lord and do good, dwell in the land and feed on His faithfulness. This Psalm makes mention of not fretting over those who do wicked things. And not to worry when it seems as if they get away with it. We are not to dwell on those who have hurt us or seem to be prospering when we are not. We are to look to God and trust in Him to take care of us and to also take care of the evil-doers.

Fretting is wearing something out—going back and forth over and over something in the mind. It is a sidetrack, instead of focusing on our lives. We will fall apart if we do this. We can't have a payback mentality toward others. We just have to trust God will take care of the wicked and those who have done us wrong. We must cease from anger and trust Him to do what He said He would do. Read Psalm 37:3-7 and write these verses out.

_____

_____

_____

_____

_____

_____

_____

_____

_____

_____

Confession

I have a new life in Christ. I am not the person I used to be. If I do mess up, I will immediately fess up and make it right. God forgives me as many times as I need forgiven because He knows my heart is to do right. I forgive myself and am free from condemnation. I make it right to anyone I offend as much as I am able to do so. By faith, I forgive those who offend me. I do not hold grudges anymore. Instead, I let go of those who have hurt me, in Jesus' name. I release them and trust the Lord to defend me and to deliver me from all my fears and troubles. I am strong in and through Him. I press on to my future. Amen.

Day #5: Read Matthew 11: 27-30. What does Jesus say in verse 28? _____

_____

_____

_____

_____

He promises us_____. In verse 29, what does He want us to do so we can stay in that rest? _____

_____

_____

_____

What is a yoke? _____

_____

Jesus says He will do a trade. He will take our burdens, cares and worries and in return He will give us His yoke, which is what? _____

1 Peter 5:6-8 says, *"Humble yourselves therefore under the mighty hand of God, that He may exalt you in due time. Casting all your care upon Him; for He careth for you. Be sober, be vigilant; because your adversary the devil, as a roaring lion, walketh about, seeking whom he may devour."*

The devil would love to devour you and get you into the pit again. But if you stay humble, daily trusting God and in right fellowship with Him, the devil can't touch you! Let God know if you are having a weak moment (since He already knows anyway) and call on Him for help. He will help you. He will deliver you from your enemies, including the enemy called addiction. He is just waiting for your permission to come into your life.

God will deliver you if you cry out for help and tell Him you're being tempted and you need help. He is an ever-present help in time of trouble—in time of your need! Or perhaps you have already messed up. You have to put on the attitude of not staying in the pit in defeat. You must get back up over and over again. You cannot quit! You cannot give up! And you cannot give in! No matter what it takes, do it! You have no choice if you want to stay clean. You've got to trust in the Lord and have rest in your soul that everything is going to be fine.

Confession

I am meek and lowly in heart. I am teachable. I want God's ways and not mine. I choose to submit to the Lord. I learn of His ways so I will become like Him. His ways are light and carefree; they are not burdensome. I don't have to be weighed down with fears and cares, but instead I can enter into His rest. He gives rest to His beloved. I am His beloved. I am able to sleep at night because I trust in Him to sustain me and deliver me from all my fears. He keeps watch over me and preserves me from evil. Everything is working out for the good in my life. He is always perfecting that which concerns me.

I am a victor in Christ. I submit myself to my Father God. I trust Him to deliver me from temptations and things that are not good for me. I refuse to worry about things, but instead I cast my cares over upon the Lord. He cares for me. He loves me and helps me as I submit to Him in all areas of my life. I have entered into His rest and put on His yoke.

Day #6: In James 4:7-8, it says to submit or humble ourselves before God and resist the devil. Then it says something amazing after that. It says when we humble ourselves and stand our ground, the devil flees from us! The devil will get as far away from you as he possibly can when he knows you mean business. We have power inside of us but we must speak it out. This is how we activate our faith. The devil doesn't want to hang around when we are talking God's Word! Try it and you will see!

First Peter 5:6-8 says that the enemy goes about like a roaring lion, seeking whom he may devour. John 10:10 says the thief comes to steal, kill and destroy. The devil is no respecter of persons. He is out to destroy mankind, particularly the children of God. But notice it says, "Whom he may devour." He can't devour you without your permission, without you giving in and quitting. So don't ever quit!

Read Daniel 6:1-28, 23. Since Daniel believed in His God, he had much favor and things worked out for him. Even though it looked like he was facing the worst possible situation, Daniel knew his God would deliver him. This is the mindset we must put on now. When we have a "no-quit" attitude, things cannot stay negative for very long! People did Daniel wrong. They lied about him, they tricked him and hated that he loved God because it made them feel guilty when they were around him. If you wonder why people in the world and even some Christians don't want to be around you, it could be a good thing! Maybe they're convicted of their sins and that is why they can't be in your presence, especially if you're always talking about Jesus. This is always a good way to get rid of carnal Christians, too—just talk about Jesus!

Not everyone is going to like us, yet we can count on God being faithful to His Word. If we will trust Him, we will make it through the trials that come our way. Read all of Acts 27. This chapter is about Paul being shipwrecked. He quoted scripture as he hung to the remains of the broken ship in the freezing water. He exhorted and encouraged others to live and not die! He trusted in God to take care of and deliver them from this bad situation. Write out verse 25 what Paul said in this situation which revealed his trust in God.

_____

_____

_____

Paul was strong in faith, knowing that God was well able to deliver Him and that He wanted to deliver him. Trust is having faith that God is going to keep His Word and help us. It's like when a child believes a parent when they say they're going to do something and the child expects them to do it. We should also expect God will do what He says!

Confession

Lord, I trust in You with all my heart. I submit to Your ways. I humble myself before You. Please help me to be strong. I will do my part, read and believe Your Word. Your words are life to me. They are health and healing to my spirit, soul and body. I take a stand for You, Jesus, and I resist all sin. I resist Satan and command him to leave me alone. I command Satan to get his hands off of my health, my wealth, my life, my family, and my future. I stand firm and choose to believe that it shall be even as God has told me it shall be. Amen.

Day #7: Read and write out your favorite verse from Psalm 91. You should memorize this whole chapter because you will definitely need to quote it often.

_____

_____

_____

_____

_____

_____

Moses wrote Psalm 91 and it is one of the most important psalms of all times. Moses had to trust God to lead over a billion of people out through the wilderness to get to their promised land. They had to go through some unpleasant situations and that generation constantly grumbled and complained. This grieved God so much, He had to wait for the next generation (their children) to rise up and dare to believe Him so He could move in their midst. You see doubt, complaining, murmuring and unbelief stopped God from being able to do anything in their lives. They cut off their own blessings! Learn from their mistakes.

Don't let God's blessings pass you by because of fear and unbelief. Ask the Lord to help you in the areas you are struggling. Humble yourself and pour your heart out to Him. Don't allow your heart to get hard like the children of Israel did in the wilderness. God meant so much more for them, but their own mouths kept them from receiving it! God could not help them because they were speaking what they believed. How sad, the first generation died never entering into the Promised Land that God had for them.

Confession

I am blessed going out and blessed coming in from now and forevermore. Wherever I go, God is with me. I am covered by the blood of the Lamb. I have a shield of protection round about me. I fear no evil. He is with me throughout the day. I can face all circumstances because I am not alone. I have the Greater One living on the inside of me. I will make it through the wilderness and the storms of this life because I choose to trust in Him to take care of me. He will get me through. I will make it to the other side. I will not die in the desert. I will enter into my promised land that God has for me. I believe it and therefore I speak it. It shall be even as He said it shall be for my life, in Jesus' name. Amen.

NOTES

_____

_____

_____

_____

_____

_____

_____

_____

_____

_____

_____

_____

_____

_____

_____

_____

_____

_____

MILESTONE #5 — USE YOUR AUTHORITY!

The fifth milestone is that I need divine intervention because I must learn how to use the authority God has given me. To do that, I must first find out what belongs to me in Christ. Then with this knowledge, I will have the power to make changes in my life and be able to say 'no' to the enemy and sin, and 'yes' to God.

John 8:32 says, *"And ye shall know the truth, and the truth shall make you free."* I also realize that I have an enemy and it is important to know how he operates. The greatest truth that I have discovered about my enemy is that he, Satan, has been defeated and I have authority over him! Jesus defeated him through the cross, burial and resurrection. When Jesus was raised from the dead, I was raised from the dead. My old life was buried with Christ. I was brought up into a new life in Him when I received Him as my Lord and Savior. Hallelujah!

I must acknowledge that not everything that goes wrong in my life is the enemy; it may be a direct result of my own fleshly desires and bad choices. Or it could be because I didn't use my authority or know I had authority to stand against and stop certain situations from happening. Perhaps I had weak boundaries and didn't know how to say 'no' to sin and unhealthy people.

When things go wrong in my life, it may be because of:

1. _____

2. _____

3. _____

Confession

I know who I am in Christ Jesus now. His blood, His Word, and His Holy Spirit are all weapons He has given to me to overcome. By faith, I have overcome drugs, alcohol and all addictions and nothing shall by any means harm me or my loved ones ever again. I am in charge of my life now! I know who I am now. I have authority! I am not powerless. All addictions must bow to the name of Jesus and leave my life forever. I am serious about staying free. I will do whatever it takes to live a holy life from this moment forward, in Jesus' name. Be gone Satan and depart from me now. I take a stand and resist you Satan. Leave me and my loved ones alone from this moment on, in Jesus' name. I submit myself to God and you must flee.

> Day #1: Today is the beginning of the rest of my life! I will not leave here like I came, in Jesus' name. I have made a decision to change and God is helping me. I am not alone. God's people are helping me. And most of all, I am helping myself! Why? Because I have been set free and intend to stay free, in Jesus' name.

Definition of authority: _____

_____

_____

_____

_____

When a policeman puts his hand up in traffic, all vehicles stop because the policeman is backed by all the authority and power of the government. The Bible says we are also backed by God's authority, the power through the blood of Christ and His Holy Word. God has given us His authority! The same power Jesus used is ours to use. We have the same rights in His name. He gave us that right when he died on the cross and descended to hell. He stripped Satan of all his power and then ascended, leaving him a defeated and powerless foe. He then gave all his rights, powers and privileges to the Church to continue His work on this earth. I am the body of Christ. I am His Church and I have all power from on high because He gave it to me! I am like Jesus on this earth. As He is, so am I!

Luke 10:18-20 18 says, *"And He said unto them, I beheld Satan as lightning fall from heaven. Behold, I give unto you power to tread on serpents and scorpions, and over all the power of the enemy: and nothing shall by any means hurt you. Notwithstanding in this rejoice not, that the spirits are subject unto you; but rather rejoice, because your names are written in heaven."*

We have authority over our enemy, the devil and his demons. We have power:

- Over our own fleshly desires, to be able to resist temptation

- To say no to unhealthy relationships and situations

- To be able to say yes to God and submit to Him

- To live our life for Christ / and for our household to be saved

- To change and be all that God wants us to be—we can in Him

Jesus said as He is, so am I in this present world. As a child of God, I have the same rights as Jesus. He died so it would be possible for me to be like Him. I am a joint heir with Christ—what belongs to Him, belongs to me! Ephesians 1:19-22 says all things have been put under His feet.

First John 4:4 says, *"Ye are of God, little children, and have overcome them: because greater is He that is in you, than he that is in the world."* When I asked Jesus to come into my life, He came to dwell inside of me and He has never left me!

How We Use Our Authority - Your Answer is in Your Mouth!

- We reverse the cycle of addiction one day at a time by using our mouths! David did not run after the giant Goliath with his mouth closed. He was on the offense and he was not quiet about it! Speak to the circumstances. Speak to yourself; say what you want your life to be like. Act and speak like Abraham did. Romans 4:17 says, "As it is written, I have made thee a father of many nations, before him whom he believed, even God, who quickeneth the dead, and calleth those things which be not as though they were."

- We train ourselves to be strong by building ourselves up through praying in the Holy Ghost and speaking God's Word. The Holy Spirit and the Word of God work together, hand in hand. (Read Romans 8 and Jude 20)

- We continue to speak the Word and send it forth like God does (Isaiah 55:11).

- The power of God can change any situation in our lives. God spoke, Jesus spoke, and now we must speak! Speaking the Word of God is our most powerful weapon. We don't wrestle against flesh and blood (people), but we take our warfare into the unseen realm of the spirit world. What takes place there manifests to the natural outside world.

- Meditate on "authority" verses. Read, memorize, and speak them out loud. Get them so ingrained in your mind and heart that God's Word will become automatic to you every time you have a weak moment. You'll counter it with the Word of God.

Jesus has done all He is ever going to do for us. Now it is our turn to act. If you don't use what He has given you, then you lose. This is a new life for you, a new way of doing things. It's your move now to do what you know to do! James 4:17 says, "Therefore to him that knoweth to do good, and doeth it not, to him it is sin." God has told you what to do—so do it!

Confession

I have authority. I have the power to say no! I have the right to tell the devil to go from my life. He is a defeated foe. Jesus defeated Satan. Satan cannot control my life now. I won't allow it! I won't allow ungodly people to dictate my life anymore. I submit myself to my Heavenly Father and He protects me and delivers me from all the plans and schemes of the enemy. Nothing shall harm me anymore. I know who I am now. I know what belongs to me now. I resist you devil and command you to stop your wicked plans in my life. I rebuke you and command you to take your hands off of my mind, my body, my family, my job, and my wealth. Everything that belongs to me and is precious and dear to me, you cannot destroy because I choose the God-kind of life. Good things happen to me now. Blessings are overtaking me. I have been delivered from the curse of the law and transferred into the kingdom of light. Jesus Christ is my Lord and Savior and all His benefits are mine.

Day #2: Read Psalm 27 and write out the verses that mean something to you.

_____

_____

_____

_____

_____

Romans 6:6-23 says we are no longer servants to sin but servants of righteousness. God has set us free, so declare that freedom. Tell yourself, tell others and tell the sin that used to dominate you. You have been delivered; for when God says He set you free, He set you free!

Romans 8:2 says, *"For the law of the Spirit of life in Christ Jesus hath made me free from the law of sin and death."* You are free from sin and death. Sin doesn't control you anymore.

Romans 8:13-14 says *"For if ye live after the flesh, ye shall die: but if ye through the Spirit do mortify the deeds of the body, ye shall live. For as many as are led by the Spirit of God, they are the sons of God."*

Mortify means to put to death. The sinful desires that were inside of you have been nailed to the cross with Jesus. They are dead. You are dead to sin and alive unto God to live for Him now. When Christ died, you died, when He rose, you arose to a new life in Him. Day by day, you are mortifying the fleshly desires of the old man. You are changing your life one day at a time—one milestone at a time! You never have to go back to the old ways ever again!

Read Romans 5 and write what it means to you: _____

_____

_____

_____

_____

_____

Confession

Today is the day the Lord has made. I will rejoice and be glad in it. Greater is He that lives in me than he that lives in the world. I fear no evil because my Father God is with me, He is in me and He will never leave me. I am not alone. I don't have to try and handle life alone anymore. The devil is exposed, the sin is exposed, the addictions are exposed and I have been set free. I will no longer run and hide or try to keep things secretive, because the more I reach out for help, the stronger I will become in Christ.

I run to the Lord because He is my light and my salvation. I have a life worth living, and I am enjoying it from this moment on. I am thankful and grateful for all that Jesus has done for me. I praise You Lord for delivering me and saving me. I have a good life to live. I am productive in the body of Christ. I have a purpose. God has a plan for my life. He made me for a purpose and I will fulfill it, one day at a time. I see things differently now because the Lord has removed the blinders from my eyes. I hear my Father God's voice, and my heart is open to receive. I choose to believe God. He will lead me and guide me. Thank You Lord! Amen.

Day #3: When I realize that I am no longer afraid,

fear has to go. It no longer has power over me. I have the power to live my life free from guilt, free from not meeting up to unrealistic expectations, free to forgive myself, free to love myself and others again. I have power and authority over my life. I am not out of control and nothing shall by any means control me again, except the Holy Spirit of God, to whom I yield myself, in Jesus' name.

My old, unrenewed mind will not control me. My body's cravings will not tell me what to do. I hear my Father God's voice, and only His voice will I obey. The Lord is my shepherd. I shall not want anything that is not good for me. I only satisfy myself with good things that are good for my soul and my body. I put off the old things, the old man, like I take off dirty, stinky clothes and I put on Christ. I put on peace. I put on love. I put on a life holy and set apart from this world's control. I put off alcohol, drugs, tobacco, unclean things and anything that would destroy who God created me to be. I put on Christ—I put on righteousness.

I am right with God and when I mess up, I repent and get back up. I get cleansed in His Holy Word and I am made clean again. I will never give up or quit. I am strong in the Lord and in the power of His might. I may not have much strength on my own, but I have Christ in me, and He said he would strengthen me and help me. God keeps His Word and watches over it in my life. So I speak my authority, in Jesus' name. I speak His Word and watch as signs and miracles follow in my life. I am so blessed! God loves me and is with me always. Today is a good day. I put on joy and choose to rejoice.

Start to laugh and laugh and laugh and watch the Holy Ghost come all over you and cause your heart to sing for joy. Rejoice! Lay hands on your heart and your head and speak the word joy. Tell your body to be joyful right now!

Read Psalm 23 and then write out your favorite scriptures from this psalm.

_____

_____

_____

_____

_____

_____

Philippians 4:13 says, "I can do all things through Christ which strengtheneth me."

What can you do now that you couldn't do before?

_____

_____

_____

_____

Nehemiah 8:10 says that the joy of the Lord is your strength. What has His joy taken the place of in your life? _____

_____

_____

Confession

I choose this day to exchange my strength for His strength. I trade my sorrows for His joy. Sadness and sorrow must flee. I choose to be glad. This is the day the Lord has made and I will be happy in it! I am not afraid of my future—He is my future now! Amen.

Day #4: In Luke 10:18, Jesus said that He saw Satan

_____.

Isaiah 14:12 and Ezekiel 28 tell us about Satan and give us a glimpse of what his job was in heaven and what happened to him. He was one of the three main angels (Gabriel- the messenger, Michael- the warrior, and Lucifer – the worshipper). He was in charge of the music, the top praise and worship leader to lead others into the throne room of God. It was an important job! That is until one day after meditating too long on himself, he decided he wanted to take God's place. He wanted to be worshipped instead of worshipping God! He liked the attention. He was the most beautiful angel ever— glorious to look upon—which puffed him up in pride. Luke 10:22 tells us that Jesus was always with the Father and He saw Satan fall as fast as lightning appears—in the blink of an eye. He was cast down so quickly!

Jesus, the Father and the Holy Spirit are one—and have always been. They are the Trinity: the three who are one: Father, Son and Holy Spirit. Now that Satan has been banned from heaven and stripped of all his privileges, he still uses music, but in a distorted way. He uses it to lead people away from God instead of drawing them to God. That is why music and drugs or any addiction go hand in hand. They feed off of each other. If you are partying, you are most likely into some kind of ungodly music that reinforces the atmosphere for the addiction to thrive—whether crying in beer country tunes that are centered on "poor ole me" or listening to heavy metal rock & roll that invites demons to the party. I know you know what I am talking about, but perhaps you never realized it until now. These are two powerful tactics of the enemy, music and addiction. The enemy uses both of these to control and ultimately destroy mankind. They have been so effective that the enemy has taken many to hell because of them. But we are not ignorant of Satan's devices. John 10:10 tells us that the thief or the snake—the devil, the wicked one, the fallen angel, Lucifer, the great deceiver—is the one who is behind it all. He does not care for the sheep! You may be thinking, Why are you telling me about the devil? Well, when you really know that your enemy was defeated and is actually powerless in your life, a confidence will rise up within you. You will begin to realize even if you don't know a lot yet about your Father God, all you have to do is say, "In Jesus' name, leave" and the devil has to go! He doesn't want to hang around and be reminded how Jesus stripped him of everything, and kicked him out of heaven and from the presence of God forever! Most of all, he doesn't want you to know!

Philippians 2:9-11 says, "Wherefore God also hath highly exalted him, and given him a name which is above every name. That at the name of Jesus every knee should bow, of things in heaven, and things in earth, and things under the earth; and that every tongue should confess that Jesus Christ is Lord, to the glory of God the Father." Everything on the earth and everything under the earth (hell) will bow to Jesus and confess Him as Lord. Everyone, everything (even addictions) must bow to the name of Jesus!

Confession

I bow my knee to the Lord Jesus Christ; He is my Lord and Savior. I confess Him as Lord. I command every part of my being to submit and bow to Jesus. My body and my mind now belong to the Lord. I have been bought with the blood of Christ. I am His now.

Day #5: Jesus became like us so that we could become like Him. He came to this earth as a man, and the Bible says He did not sin. He was tempted in all areas like we are. He knows mankind's weaknesses. He said that we can overcome. He said He wasn't going to take us out of the world, but would give us the strength to live in it and be a witness for Him. He has given us all power and everything we will ever need to stand strong.

I believe God at His Word. I am strong in the Lord and the power of His might. By faith I live one day at a time. I walk it out—one day at a time!

Read Ephesians 6:10-17 about the whole armor of God and write out the pieces of it. _____

_____

_____

_____

_____

_____

_____

_____

Confession

God gave me armor to cover every area of my life. He's got me covered! He covers my feet for the places I walk, my thought life by putting on His helmet, a sword to be on the offense, a shield when I have to be on the defensive to cover and protect me, and a breastplate for guarding my heart and protecting most of me. The belt of truth is wrapped around me to support me and gird my mind with truth that keeps me free. I know who I am in Christ Jesus now. I am set free and Satan is a defeated foe with no rights to my life!

> Day #6: Joseph fled some uncomfortable situations that would have caused him to mess up. The Bible says he fled from his master's wife when she tempted him to sin. He even left the place naked when she tried to seduce him (Read Genesis 39.) This is how we must respond, we must flee at whatever cost, anything that tries to trip us up or pull us back into sin.

We do not have control over other people, but we can get away from them. Ephesians 6:12 says, "For we wrestle not against flesh and blood, but against principalities, against powers, against the rulers of the darkness of this world, against spiritual wickedness in high places." Jesus said He has put all things—including the devil—under His feet, therefore under our feet! Read Ephesians 1:22-23.

You have Satan under your feet because of Jesus. You have God's power in you to tell the temptations, the devil and all evil where to go! So do it! Speak it, believe it, and act like it is so! Ephesians 5:18 says, "And be not drunk with wine, wherein is excess; but be filled with the Spirit." It says to be drunk on the new wine, so start praising the Lord in the Spirit. The devil can't stand to be around you when you pray in tongues! He just has a fit because He can't penetrate or interrupt your personalized prayer life. Praying in the Spirit and being full of the Word of God will help you flee from unsafe situations. The Holy Spirit will give you discernment to know when to flee fast if you have to get out of there. God will deliver you from people, places, and things that are entrapments of the enemy to bring you down.

Confession

I do not fight against flesh and blood; my battle is in the unseen world against the powers of darkness. I am not afraid of them because Jesus already defeated Satan and all of his cohorts. I bind all demoniac assignments planned against me and command them to come to naught! No weapon formed against me will prevail. Greater is He, Jesus, that lives in me than he that is in this world.

I fear no evil for the Lord is with me and on my side. No evil will befall me. I am covered in the blood of Jesus. I continually remind the devil about the blood of Christ and how he is a defeated. All sin is under my feet, Satan and his demons are under my feet. I am victorious through Christ Jesus, my Lord. I don't need this world's intoxication. All I need is the high of the Most High. I get drunk on the new wine now! I am drunk on the Holy Ghost!

Day #7: All God's promises are 'Yes' and 'Amen!' He blesses me and makes a way when there seems to be no way. He will perfect that which concerns me. James 1 says that every good and perfect gift comes down from above. Acts 10:38 says that Jesus went around doing good, healing all that were oppressed of the devil. He delivers me! Amen.

We can know that God wants us to have good things in our lives, but knowing is not enough. You will have to go after it and demand the devil to loose what belongs to you. Tell him to get his hands off of your property! Tell him he will not destroy your life with addictions or anything else. Bind him from being able to do any more damage. You do have the right and the power backing you! So what are you going to do about it? All authority has been given to you. You have control to change your destiny. Your life doesn't have to remain the same. Whatsoever we allow, it shall be. But whatsoever we do not allow —it cannot be!

We possess the power to bind and loose the enemy in our lives and in the lives of those who are in our care, under our authority. Read Matthew 18:18-20. Write out the verses that have meaning to you. _____

_____

_____

_____

_____

_____

_____

_____

_____

_____

Write out what you want to bind the enemy from in your life

and declare it so: _____

_____

_____

_____

_____

_____

_____

_____

_____

_____

_____

_____

If you want things to change—declare them changed! Make it happen! That is your God-given right. Don't allow sickness to come in and destroy your life. Don't allow addictions to control you anymore. Don't allow unclean people to control you any longer. Say, "No!" Tell the devil where to go, in Jesus' name! Just saying 'no' works when you're empowered by God!

Write out John 14: 13-14. _____

_____

_____

_____

_____

_____

_____

_____

_____

_____

_____

People often wonder how they can stop the devil in other peoples' lives such as their loved ones, since they have a free will. You can't control another person's free will, and God can't either. If He could, He would make us all get saved and do right! But we have authority over what is ours and what goes on in our households. It is our territory and our domain, so we have the right to speak into our children's lives and bind the enemy from them. We have the right to break the controlling powers of Satan over our loved ones so they can receive from God.

3 Ways We Can Pray and Use Our Authority

- Command the god of this world to loose them and let them go! Command the eyes of their understanding be enlightened so they can see clearly, instead of being deceived. Tell the scales to be removed from their eyes, in Jesus' name.

- You have authority over anyone or anything that belongs to you: your home, your finances, your job, and your children. Cover it all with the blood of Jesus and command the enemy to leave them because they are not under his authority; they are under yours! Take charge and do not allow sin in your home anymore. You have dominion in your realm or territory. Your children are marked with the same bloodline—the blood of Christ. The enemy can't have them! Claim their lives for Christ and they will not be able to connect with the wrong associates, places or things. They will be most miserable until they surrender to Jesus Christ and make Him Lord of their lives.

- Continue to push back the darkness in every area of your life by speaking the Word of God daily and declaring what you desire. You may say, "Well, it may not be God's will for me to prosper. It may not be God's will for my family to be with me." But if you desire these things and you are a child of God living for Him and in tune with His voice, doesn't He say He will give you the desires of your heart? Dare to believe it and receive it! If it is in the Bible, it is God's will for you. Remember, if it is good, it is God. If it is evil, it is not of God. James 1:17 says, "Every good gift and every perfect gift is from above, and cometh down from the Father of lights, with whom is no variableness, neither shadow of turning."

NOTES

_____

_____

_____

_____

_____

_____

_____

_____

_____

_____

_____

MILESTONE #6 — PRAISE AND WORSHIP IN RECOVERY

The sixth milestone is to accept that I need divine intervention in the area of music and other areas that feed my emotions. As I sing and praise, I'm learning that this is a way to receive God's power into my life and heal my soul. Praise is the highest form of prayer that I can offer to God. I love to praise the Lord because when I do so, I focus on the goodness of God instead of my problems. Praising God causes fear and cares to flee from me. Therefore, I choose to praise the Lord! When I awake in the morning, I will praise Him. In the afternoon, I will praise Him. And in the evening, I will praise Him. In other words, I will praise Him all the day long, 24/7!

God loves to inhabit the praises of His people. I invite Father God into my life by praising Him. His Holy presence overtakes me and causes my heart and soul to be flooded with peace. There is no fear in His presence. There are no worries or cares in His presence. I love to sing praises to my Father and be with His people. This is who I am now. This is my new life. I do not fear the future, because He is my future. Addictions no longer control me—they are under my feet! They no longer have any influence in my life. Hallelujah!

Music is an effective tool in recovery. It connects you to and creates an atmosphere of the world that you want to inhabit.

Remember the Tasmanian Devil in the Warner Brothers cartoons with Bugs Bunny? The music actually calmed down the wild beast and made him peaceful, however Bugs used it to manipulate him.

Music has power over the soul realm. It feeds the emotions. Our soul consists of our thoughts, emotions, and our will. Whatever our soul is full of is who we are and what we do. The will is the decision maker, determining which direction our body will go and what it will do. What is in one's soul will manifest to his outer man. That's why music meditation is so powerful and has great influence. It has the potential within it to steer the course of one's life. If you don't change your music after you get clean and sober, there will still be a longing in the soul realm to drag you back into that world of addictions. Don't underestimate music's power!

The world's music worships man and not God. Its words are powerful, and you don't want to go around confessing the wrong thing over and over. When you sing, you are making a confession with your mouth. Romans 10:9-10 says, "That if thou shalt confess with thy mouth the Lord Jesus, and shalt believe in thine heart that God hath raised him from the dead, thou shalt be saved. For with the heart man believeth unto righteousness; and with the mouth confession is made unto salvation." As a man thinketh in his heart, so is he—he will live and do what he has been meditating on!

For example, the song "Joker" by the Steve Miller Band which I was familiar with in my hippie days, seems to be playing on the radio again. It has great guitar sounds, but the words speak of smoking weed. "What is going to be on your mind and coming out of your mouth if you sing that song? Getting high! It has a catchy beat, but listen to the words! Is that your confession? You're a smoker and a midnight toker? I hope not!

Or what about Eric Clapton's song, "Cocaine". He is singing about having an affair with a lethal drug. You better not be saying "she" is the answer! How many lives have been destroyed because some young person thought it was cool to meditate on this song and then ended up strung out? And guess what? Yes, she does lie! Of course, the devil is the ultimate liar behind it all. Cocaine does lie. It destroys lives and brings many blues. Remember, music is one of the most powerful forms of meditation!

Man first thinks on music, then speaks what he is going to do before he does it. That's why the songs we sing need to take us in a different direction than where the world is going. And whatever used to be our party music, cannot be our music now. Our music needs to be substituted with good music—words that lift up God, edify your spirit man and feed your soul – this needs to be your new meditation. Such songs are uplifting and have great guitar tunes as well!

When I hear a song from my B.C. days (Before Christ), I can tell you exactly what I was doing, where I was, and how I was feeling during that time. Most likely, it was getting high or doing something that had me in bondage. These songs boxed me into their world and then I reinforced those things by singing the songs. I created my own prison. But Praise God, He got me out! Only Jesus could get me out, because I was in so deep. Now, I will do whatever it takes to stay out and stay free.

I'm not against music. Music plays an important role in my family's life. Two of my sons are musicians and songwriters. Our house is usually full of someone jamming on the guitar or beating the drums. We need to listen to the spirit behind the music and the words. Think about what atmosphere the music you listen to is trying to create in your life. And always ask yourself if this is a song that leads you to God or away from Him. Especially if a song conjures up old memories, you need to choose a different tune!

> Day #1: Today is the beginning of the rest of my life! I will not leave here like I came, in Jesus' name. I have made a decision to change, and God will help me. I am not alone. God's people will help me. And most of all, I will help myself because I have been set free and I intend to stay free! Amen.

What is praise?

1. Praise is the highest form of prayer.

2. Praise is making a show of celebration, shouting, clapping and throwing up ones' hands.

3. Praise is kneeling in adoration, singing hymns of worship, and confessing the goodness of God.

4. Praise is making music by striking an instrument or one's hands.

Psalm 40:3 says, "And he hath put a new song in my mouth, even praise unto our God: many shall see it, and fear, and shall trust in the LORD."

Many will be amazed what God has done in your life and will turn to and trust in the Lord. Psalm 8:2 says, "Out of the mouth of babes and sucklings hast thou ordained strength because of thine enemies, that thou mightest still the enemy and the avenger."

He has ordained praise to do what? _____

_____

_____

_____

Do you need to shut the devil up? Then sing to the Lord. The devil can't stand to be around worshippers! A worshipper is not swayed by this world's tunes. He hears his Father's voice and follows no other. He hears the beat of a different drum!

In the last days, this generation of God's army will consist of true worshippers. God wants us to be worshippers. Praise and worship comfort and sustain us when the storms of life come. Read 2 Chronicles 20:15-22. This chapter talks about how Jehoshaphat sent the worshippers out ahead of the army. The singers marched out first worshipping God. It confused the enemy so much that it caused them to turn on each other in fear. They began attacking each other and were destroyed. They left behind all their goods and valuables—the spoils they had stolen from others!

God's people never had to fight in a physical battle, God did that! He had them fighting in the spiritual world by singing and worshipping. This silenced the enemy and caused them to be in a state of confusion, ultimately destroying each other. And when it was all over with, God told them to go into the enemy's camp and collect all the spoils of the enemy. Now that is a "more than a conqueror" battle! God did all the work and they reaped all the goods! When you don't know what to do and all pressure is coming at you, stop and praise Him. Then watch Him turn things around in your life.

When we praise God, we are surrounded by His presence and He fights our battles for us! He sets up ambushes against the enemy. When you don't know what to do and are facing temptations, troubles and worries—stop and praise before you do anything else. Watch God move on your behalf because He loves the praises of His people and it stirs Him into action on your behalf.

When you want a drink or want to get a fix, stop and praise

instead! Cry out to God for His help. Tell the devil where to go, withstand him. Then put on some worship music and begin to praise and sing to the Lord of lords and the King of kings! I guarantee that as you take a stand, you will forget all about getting high because you will be experiencing the "real thing," the Most High!

Ambushment means _____

_____

_____

_____

Philippians 4:4 tells us to: _____

_____

Regardless of our situation, if we stop and praise the Lord before we allow all the cares, fears and worries to overwhelm us, we will come out victorious every time. This is vital in recovery. You cannot afford to allow discouragement to come in because it will eat away at you and destroy you. It will take you backwards! You have to choose to put on a merry heart and that comes through knowing that you are forgiven and who you are in Christ. Then put on an attitude of gratitude; it will take you to a new altitude. It will take you up higher above the circumstances so you can see clearly above the storm.

Ephesians 5:19-20 tells us we are to make melody in our hearts. Have you ever noticed a person who goes around singing all day? He is usually a happy-go -lucky person. And that person doesn't lack friends, because people want to be around someone who is uplifting and positive. How many people do you see positive in this negative world? It can be a rarity!

James 5:16 says, "The effectual fervent prayer of a righteous man availeth much." Our prayers avail much. Your prayers do matter.

God hears your prayers. You can count on it when you are praying accordingly to His will. His will is to heal, to deliver, to set free, and to transform lives. His will is to forgive sins. His will is that we never see Hell. His will is for us to live a productive life on earth and have all of our needs met. God is a good God! His will is for us to live in peace.

Confession

I rejoice in the Lord knowing He takes good care of me. I will not fear; I will not care. Instead, I cast all my cares over on Him. I trust in Him to keep His Word. I rejoice, knowing that God is taking care of every situation in my life. He is restoring everything back to me that the enemy meant to destroy. He gives me life, and life more abundantly! My Father God is with me. He is for me and He lives in me. He will never abandon me nor forsake me. He helps me. I love Him and I praise Him from now and forever more. I worship Him with my mind, my body, and all that is within me. I bless His Holy name. I will sing of His mercies all the day long. I choose to have a joyful heart of worship and sing to Him continuously. I watch and see as my life changes and things turn around. Amen.

Day #2: In the midnight hour, God's going to turn it around! I know that God will work everything out for my good. My life is in His hands and I praise Him—no matter how I feel, no matter what I think, no matter what the situation looks like. I praise Him for He is my Lord! This is the day that He has made and I will rejoice in it. I know things are going to get better because God has lifted me up out of the pit. He has good plans for my

life! I believe it. I receive it, in Jesus' name. No longer
will I stay down. I am lifted up above my enemies and
my feet are now established on solid ground. Even in
the darkest situations, I will make it through because
I am not alone. God is with me and He is for me. He
lives in me. Hallelujah!

Read Acts 16. Paul and Silas were in jail singing praises to
God. The whole jail began to shake like an earthquake as they were
released by God's angels. Miraculous things happen when you praise
the Lord. Even in the midst of your troubled situation, God will set up
ambushments against your enemies. He will deliver you!

What do you need God to deliver you from or help you with?

By faith, thank Him for delivering you from these. Read Acts
27. Notice how Paul handles being in a shipwreck. This is another
example of how to act when it looks like everything is going wrong.
Remember, we don't live according to this world's system. We are not
moved by how we feel. Only the Word of God moves us. Even when we
are in the storm, we will not sink. He is with us, and He will deliver
us! We will meditate on His Word and praise His name even in the
midst of storms and shipwrecks. You may say, "That is crazy!" Yes, it
is! But try it, and see how God will turn things around for you. Watch
how He will move on your behalf!

Confession

Lord, there is no situation impossible or too hard for You. I choose
to trust in You and praise You for the victory even before I can see it.
I know You always deliver Your children. You are the provider. You
are El Shaddai, the God who is more than enough. I trust in You. You

are my shield and protector, I will not fear.

You are my healer. You are the healer of broken hearts; You are the healer and the restorer of life. You replace death with life. You replace sickness with health. You replace darkness with life. You replace confusion, chaos and fear with peace and tranquility.

You are the Great I Am! I dare to believe You when I don't know what to do. You always watch over Your Word to perform it. I will continue to speak Your Word and not my own understanding and thoughts. I choose to see beyond the storm. I will make it to the other side, in Jesus' name. I will come through these storms! To You be all the glory, honor and praise in my life. Amen.

> Day #3: When King David was discouraged or depressed, he would speak to his mind and tell it to be quiet and bless the Lord instead! He voiced his problems and acknowledged that they were real. Then he spoke the scriptures to himself, encouraging himself until he was happy in the Lord. He refused to stay in a state of self-pity. So must you! Refuse to stay down.

Write out and speak out loud Psalm 103:1-3:

_____

_____

_____

_____

_____

_____

_____

_____

_____

_____

_____

_____

_____

_____

_____

_____

What are four benefits that God has given you?

_____

_____

_____

_____

Now read all of Psalm 103 and select a favorite verse. Write it out and memorize it.

_____

_____

_____

_____

_____

_____

_____

_____

Confession

God has forgiven me of my sins. He has healed me of all sicknesses and diseases. He has delivered me from addictions. He has put a new song in my heart. He has healed my mind and given me new thoughts. I can dare to dream again! I am a new person in Christ Jesus. I am not the same person I used to be, because Christ has set me free. I choose to rejoice and be happy. I choose to think on the goodness of God, rather than the fears and cares of this world. I will sing and make melodies to the Lord. I will worship Him because He loves me and cares for me. I am not alone. He is with me and will never leave me. Amen.

Day #4: Read Jonah 2:1-10. Jonah tried to run away from the call of God on his life and he ended up in a bad situation. But then he remembered his God and began to sing in the belly of the whale. He was in the lowest of low places. He probably was left for dead. Who would have thought he was still alive? It looked like a "no-way out situation," yet he began to praise God. The Lord heard his cry and delivered him. The giant fish had to spit him out. He couldn't stay in that mess! Praise will not keep you down or let you remain stuck in a situation.

Jonah brought this on himself because he was disobedient and ran away from God. Yet, when he cried out in repentance, God instantly delivered him and turned everything around for him. Of course, he still had to do what God told him to do. If you read on, Jonah became a mighty man of God to the people of Nineveh. They believed in mermaids, and what did God do? He had Jonah spat out of a giant fish and the people saw it! They were amazed and thought some deity came to visit them. I think God has a sense of humor. He used the very thing they worshipped to reach them. God met them where they were. Jonah told them about the one true God. The Bible says everyone repented of their idols and turned away from sin.

What pit do you need God to deliver you out of? _____

_____

_____

_____

_____

_____

_____

_____

_____

_____

Confession

I have turned my life over to the Lord. Today is the day the Lord has made! I am happy in it. I am covered in the blood of Jesus and I am saved. I do not run from God; I run to Him. I will not run from situations that make me uncomfortable. Instead, I will stand and be strong in the Lord. He is my helper. I am not alone. I can and will make it with His help. I will repent when I need to and get back up. I will never quit or give up. Where would I go? Who would I turn to? God is my only hope. I will praise the Lord with all my being, all the breath that is within me will sing of His wonderful works. I choose to be thankful. I thank You, Lord, for always being there for me and never giving up on me.

Day #5: Read Psalm 136. Praise the Lord, for His mercy endureth forever is what it says over and over. This is a victory song that the children of Israel would sing repeatedly in their time of worship to the Lord. They were commanded to say this! Then they watched God deliver them in a mighty way. They chanted this verse: The Lord is good and His mercies endure forever and ever. Say this seven times to yourself. When you don't know what to say, when you don't know what to pray— take a stand and praise Him. In 2 Chronicles 20:21, the worshippers chanted this under the instruction of King Jehoshaphat. On the seventh day and the seventh time that the children of Israel marched around Jericho, they probably shouted Psalm 136, the battle cry chant, "The Lord is good and His mercies endure forever!" When they obeyed, the walls of that fortified city came crashing down! The same will happen for you when you sing and praise Him!

As you praise the Lord, watch the walls in your life come tumbling down. What seemed like mountains of problems will disappear when you praise the Lord! Mark 11:23 tells us to speak to the mountains and they will be cast into the sea. Speak to those huge mountains of problems and watch them disappear! Keep speaking the desired result, even when things are difficult all around you and you want to scream or maybe even check out, get another drink or get high. Don't give in, just stop and say a faith confession instead. Replace the temptation with the praises of the Lord!

Confession

I was made for praise and that is what I will do today! I have control over my body. I have control over my thoughts and emotions. I choose to bless the Lord with all my soul and all that is within me. I praise the name of Jesus, the name that is above all other names. Everyone must bow to the name of Jesus! You are good, O Lord, and Your mercies endure forever and ever. I am going to make it through this day. You deliver me from situations that are too hard for me and I can't handle on my own. You are my helper. You are my strong tower and I run to you. I am safe from all the cares and fears of this life. I cast them over onto you. You care for me and make a way when there seems to be no way. I can't carry this load, and I won't anymore. By faith, I give it to You, my Heavenly Father and ask You to take care of it for me, in Jesus' name, I pray. Amen.

Day#6: Most of the psalms were songs sung to the Lord and written by David. Find your favorite psalm and turn it into your own private worship. Psalm 91 was written by Moses during the time when he led the children of Israel out of Egypt. Egypt was a type of the world without God. The Promised Land that they were headed into was a type of God's blessing and provision on the earth.

God calls His people out to a place that they do not know and plants and establishes them in a new place. Read Hebrews 11:8 where it talks about Abraham obeying God, leaving all his possessions behind when he didn't know where he was going. Yet, he ventured on because he fully trusted the Lord. It would be beneficial to memorize Psalm 91, because you will probably be praying it every day of your life—whether for protection, deliverance or just in worship. This psalm must become one of your prayers. For example, in verse 2 it says, "I will say of the Lord He is my refuge and my fortress. My God in Him will I trust."

Find a psalm that has meaning to you, write it out and meditate on it.

_____

_____

_____

_____

_____

_____

_____

_____

_____

_____

_____

Confession

Where God leads, I will follow. I am not afraid of the unknown, because I am in good hands. I am in the palm of His hand. He cares for me. He protects me, He shows me what is to come, and I will obey. I am not afraid to go forward and leave all. If God asks me to give up something, it is because He has something even better for me down the road. So I choose to trust and obey Him. The Bible says if I am willing and obedient, I will eat the good of the land. I am willing and obedient. I hear the voice of the Good Shepherd and I do follow.

> Day # 7: Psalm 89:1-18 invites worship to the Lord. This was a song or a dialectic poem of old that we can still sing today. Dialect means having a conversation with each other or to God. Sing to the Lord! You may say, "I can't sing." Well, then do it in your closet or shower! Singing to God lifts you up and awakens your spirit man. Your spirit loves to praise God.

What do you think we will be doing in heaven? We will be worshipping—and we will be loving it, too! So we should start practicing while we are still here on the earth. Verse 1 says, "I will sing of the mercies of the Lord." Praising God is an act of your will. At times, you have to make yourself do it. With our mouths, we will make known His faithfulness to our generation. How can we be quiet after all God has done for us and continues to do for us? The Bible says if we don't praise Him then the rocks will cry out. Well, I don't want any rocks outdoing me! Do you? All creation will praise Him forever and ever. Read the rest of Psalm 89 and personalize it. Talk back to God with His Word. He loves it!

Confession

This is the day to praise. I will get my mind off of myself and I will look to the Lord. He is an ever-present help in time of need. He is my rock and my hiding place. I can run to Him and retreat. When others around me don't care or don't understand, I can run to my Father God who is always there. He is as close as the mention of His name. I am surrounded by His angels. I am safe and protected from all harm. I rejoice knowing my Father God has me in the palms of His hand. What a day I will have today as I let my light shine in this dark world and sing the praises of my Lord. The Lord helps me to make a difference in the lives of those around me. So I will let my light shine. Amen.

NOTES

_____

_____

_____

_____

_____

_____

_____

_____

_____

_____

_____

_____

_____

_____

_____

_____

_____

_____

MILESTONE #7 — LIVING ON SOLID GROUND

The seventh milestone is to admit I need divine intervention in my life so I can start living a life of stability and peace. I desire to live on solid ground now and get established in Christ. I no longer want to live in a crisis mode! I will not stress out at every whim and whoa! Not everything is an emergency. And if I don't get my way, it is okay. Life is not all about me, myself, and I. Other people are affected by my choices, and I will start considering the whole picture and not my world only. Things are changing in my life for the better.

When things begin to overwhelm me, I will run to my Father God. I will make myself stop; I will silence the enemy by praising my Father God for His goodness in my life. I will not run back to the bottle, drugs or unhealthy relationships. I will not run to the mall and charge up things I really don't need. I will not go into some self-destructive mode and become reckless in my living. I will not stew in self-pity and pet addictions. I will not stress my loved ones out. Instead, I will stop and breathe. I will think before I speak. I will pray before I act. I will not live on the edge anymore. I will not be on the defensive and ready to react and explode. I have self-control now. The things that triggered me before do not have control over me anymore.

Day #1: Today is the beginning of the rest of my life! I will not leave here like I came, in Jesus' name. I have made a decision to change and God will help me. I am not alone. God's people will help me. And most of all, I will help myself! Because I have been set free, I intend to stay free! Amen.

Matthew 7:24 says, "Therefore whosoever heareth these sayings of mine, and doeth them, I will liken him unto a wise man, which built his house upon a rock: And the rain descended, and the floods came, and the winds blew, and beat upon that house; and it fell not: for it was founded upon a rock." Our desire and mission is that you become that house founded and built on the Rock—Christ Jesus so when the storms of life come your way (and they will come), you will still be standing! But there is something you must do. According to Matthew 7:24, you must _____

_____.

God will do His part when we make the first move and do our part. It's like in a game of Chess. You make a move, God makes a move, and then it's your move again. God is not playing games with you, but He does expect you to do something.

Rains, floods and storms all represent: _____

_____

In Matthew 7:24-27, what happens to the man who hears God's Word and doesn't do it? _____

_____

_____

_____

_____

The house in this story represents what? _____

_____

The Bible is always about two men: the one

who_____ and the one who_____

_____

_____.

Obedience =_____

_____

Disobedience = _____

_____

There are two kinds of people in the world. There are the ones who make it in life by conquering situations and by not giving up. They persevere and press forward. Even in impossible situations, they won't quit! Then there are those who allow their lives to beat them up. Circumstances dominate them, causing them to fail over and over again until they are not able to get back up on their own. Then they get mad at God and blame Him, along with blaming others, too. When a lot of times it was their own poor choices that put them in these unpleasant situations in the first place!

James 1:22 says, "But be ye doers of the word, and not hearers only, deceiving your own selves."

Read all of James 1 and meditate on these verses. Write out what God is saying to you in these scriptures. _____

_____

_____

_____

_____

_____

_____

_____

_____

Do you want stability? God promises us stability in His Word over and over again. If we serve Him and study His Word, He will anchor us to His will and nothing will be able to sway us or cause us to fall away from it.

Isaiah 33:6 says, "And wisdom and knowledge shall be the stability of thy times, and strength of salvation."

Knowledge is when you learn a truth. Wisdom is when you apply that truth to your life. It's not enough to just hear good information. You must weave it into your life to make it a part of everything you do. This will bring stability for your times—for your life and what you're going through. Hosea 4:6 says, "My people are destroyed for lack of knowledge." Lack of knowledge implies the things they don't know or they know and don't do.

We all go through "stuff," but it is the man who is still standing during the storm and has the Word of God in Him, who will make it to the other side. He will have the guts to press on no matter how hard things get. He will have an "I will not quit," and an "I cannot be defeated" attitude. This is what we all need to have in order to make it. We must be aggressive in recovery or we won't be standing on solid ground—and we'll get stuck in sinking sand.

Confession

I have the mind of Christ. I am His child. His Spirit is in me. He calms me. In Him I run and hide. He is my shelter; He is my hiding place. I am safe in Him. I am a new creation in Him; old things have passed away and all things are new in my life. I am not afraid. I am growing in God, day by day. I am not the person I was yesterday. I am getting established and rooted in Christ. He is my rock and my fortress. People can't jerk my chain. I won't go so far and always be pulled back.

I am like a tree with my roots deep in the Word of God. I know who I am now. I can't be swayed, and I will not run away! I am founded on the rock so when the storms of life come, I will still be standing. Jesus is my rock! He is my firm foundation. He will help me and hold me up with His right hand of righteousness. Hallelujah! Amen.

Day #2: He has delivered me from all my fears. I trust in Him with all my heart and I lean not to my own understanding. I now submit my life over to the care of my Father God. He cares for me and loves me. He will help me today. He leads me and guides me in the decisions I make. I will not mess up like I have in the past. I have favor now. I have favor with God, therefore He gives me favor with man and cause all things to work together for my good. He blesses me and makes a way when there seems to be no way.

This day, I will praise and thank God. It is a glorious day! I receive His strength, and I can do all things because He empowers me with strength. He gives me wisdom to know which way to go and which way not to turn. I hear His voice and all other voices must be silenced, in Jesus' name. I command my mind to think on God's thoughts. I choose to have an attitude of gratitude. I am very thankful and humble that God loves me and has given me a second chance in life. Thank you Lord. Amen.

Psalm 40:2 says, "He brought me up also out of a horrible pit, out of the miry clay, and set my feet upon a rock, and established my goings." (This is a process!)

We all have been in terrible pits, but God delivers us from them all! The clay means we were stuck really solid. It looked like a "no way out" situation. Miry means slimy, rotten and stinky – like a stagnant dried up pond. Yuk! The Greek actually says that miry means a well of intoxication. He pulled us up out of that well of slimy, stinky, rotten intoxication. It was so slippery that we couldn't get out on our own, so He pulled us out with His mighty hand and then out of the next layer of the clay, delivered us from the hardness of our hearts and the "stuck" circumstances.

After He delivered us, He planted us, establishing us in His root system so we could become settled and grounded in Him. Our feet got placed on a rock (Him) so now we can look up and see that He really does have a purpose for our lives. Only God could break through the years and layers of muck and break it off of us. We couldn't do it by ourselves. We still need His help daily and as we humble ourselves and ask for His help, He will help us! He will break the years of our old ways and our old manipulative mindsets—the old man—off of us. Then He will put a new song in our hearts.

He will set us free so we feel like we could run around a block or leap over a wall. That's why you see people jumping up and down. Don't be so quick to judge them. You don't know what kind of pit they were in before God set them free. He will do the same for you. Jump up and down right now if you dare! Just laugh, thank Him, and watch the heaviness flee. Oppression cannot stay when you praise God. He sets our feet upon something solid so we won't slip and sink back into our old lifestyles. His Word becomes our stability and it establishes our goings. Hallelujah!

From what pit did God bring you out? _____

_____

_____

_____

_____

_____

_____

_____

How are things stable in your life now? What steps are you taking to make it happen? _____

_____

_____

_____

_____

_____

_____

_____

What three areas do you need to work on? _____

_____

_____

_____

_____

_____

_____

_____

_____

_____

Day #3: Today, I am quick to listen and slow to speak. I am quick to repent and slow to get angry. I am quick to forgive and I am calm and at peace. Nothing or no one jerks my chain, pulls my triggers or causes me to react. I take full responsibility for my actions. I will not lose self-control and get angry, because this does not promote the righteousness of God in my life. People won't see Jesus in me when I dwell in the flesh. They need to see me changed so it will give them hope in a miracle-working God. He has set me free; He has healed me and delivered me. I will let the world know it by my lifestyle. I don't have to try and prove things to people by telling them; I just live my life and let the light of Christ shine through me. It is marvelous in His sight! I am not the person I used to be. I am a new creation in Christ Jesus, my Lord. The past is gone and my future is ever before me. I am obtaining it one day at a time—one milestone at a time. Amen.

James 1:19-22 says, "Wherefore, my beloved brethren, let every man be swift to hear, slow to speak, slow to wrath: For the wrath of man worketh not the righteousness of God. Wherefore lay apart all filthiness and superfluity of naughtiness, and receive with meekness the engrafted word, which is able to save your souls. But be ye doers of the word, and not hearers only, deceiving your own selves."

The Word is implanted in us. God does spiritual surgery on our hearts and minds. He puts something inside of us that was taken out when Adam sinned in the Garden. When we receive Jesus, we get it all back. We become what we were supposed to be all along, before mankind had ever sinned. Reading and speaking the Word of God anchors our souls and nothing is able to shake us anymore. It's not like before! The more His Word is implanted in us, the more we will grow strong in Him. Then we will start taking on that conquering mentality of Jesus Christ, who is the King of kings and the Lord of all lords. Amen.

Read, pray and write out Ephesians 3:14-21. _____

_____

_____

_____

_____

_____

_____

_____

_____

_____

_____

_____

_____

_____

_____

God wants to strengthen you. He wants you to get grounded, rooted and established. He doesn't want you tossed around anymore.

The more you realize His love for you, the more you will become secure and stable in Him. The more you trust God, the more you will understand His love for you. You will be filled with the knowledge of His love and you will be able to believe that all things are possible. He wants to give you the desires of your heart— exceedingly, abundantly above all you can ask, hope, dream or desire. Ask Him for what you need and want. He says you have not because you ask not.

As long as it is according to His will, you can count on it that He wants you to have it. His will is salvation, His will is getting filled with the Holy Spirit and being strengthened from on high, His will is for you to be in health and that your soul prospers, His will is for you to have a sound mind, His will is for you to be totally delivered from all addictions. So when things try to dominate you, you can operate out of your own free will. God doesn't want to control you. He wants you to be in control of your life and have stability. This is true freedom!

Day #4: Read and write out Colossians 1:23. _____

_____

_____

_____

_____

_____

I am not tossed to and fro. I know what the will of the Lord is for my life. I am grounded and settled in Him now. I am established in Christ. I continue in the faith and I am becoming stronger day by day because of it. Amen.

Colossians 2:6-7 says, "As ye have therefore received Christ Jesus the Lord, so walk ye in him: Rooted and built up in him, and stablished in the faith, as ye have been taught, abounding therein with thanksgiving."

As you have been taught by your brothers and sisters in Christ, as you have been taught by the Word of God, as you have been taught by the Holy Spirit of God, continue in the faith. Don't quit. Don't give up and never give in! Then you will become stable and grounded. There will be stuff that happens that may be a real crisis, but you will be okay. You won't fall apart because you are in Christ and you are settled in Him. You know that your Father God is going to take care of you and deliver you from all harm and evil. Be thankful and rejoice! You have so much to be thankful for. You were dead and now you are alive unto God!

Read Ephesians 2: 1- 10. After reading these verses, fill in the blanks here:

I was in my trespasses and _____. I was once a

son or child of _____ but now I am a child of God.

God was so rich in His _____ towards

me. Because He _____ me so. I was dead in

_____, but He made me _____ in Christ

(Verse 8). I was saved through _____. It was not

anything I could have done on my own. Even that faith was a

_____ from God to me. He loved me that much!

It was not of my _____ lest I would boast and

say look what I have done. My works could never get me into

heaven. It was the work of _____ that saved

me. I am His workmanship created to do works now.

Confession

I hear my Father's voice and the voice of the stranger, I will not follow. I flee youthful lusts. I stay away from people, places, and things that would interfere with my sobriety and walk with God. No weapon formed against me will prosper, in word or deed. But whatever I do will succeed. Every tongue that rises up against me, I forgive and prove to be in the wrong by my godly lifestyle (Isaiah 54:17). God fights my battles now. I don't have to go around trying to prove myself to anyone. I live one day at a time in the love and forgiveness of my Father, God. He loves me. He loved me so much He gave His Son to die for me. I will in turn, give my life to Him. I forgive as He has forgiven me. I love as He has loved me.

> Day #5: Read Psalm 1: 1-8. Then write out the verses that mean something to you. Psalm 1 is a chapter that should be memorized. It is about a man; it could be anyone of us. He is walking down the road of life. There will always be those in our pathway who will say, "Come this way, come do this, or come do that," and if we don't know who we are, we can get so easily swayed—especially when it is something that we really want. Maybe you want to be accepted and fit in with the crowd. Maybe you just want a friend. There is nothing wrong with that, but it is very important that the company you choose are godly companions because they will influence your walk tremendously and take you down their pathway.

Backsliding is turning away from God. This "slipping" is such a sly process that we don't see it coming a lot of times. It starts out with you walking down the road of life and up ahead there are some friends saying, "Here is a shortcut," but it's a pathway you know you should avoid. But maybe you are hungry, angry, lonely, or just plain tired—H.A.L.T. as they say in Alcoholics Anonymous. Your guard is down and you just need someone to talk to who understands. And so you go a route you should not travel. Stop and think about these H.A.L.T. triggers before you go any further.

When you are in any one of these situations, your guard will be down so you could be sucked back in so easily. Don't do something you will regret. It could take you a long time to recover, if you ever do recover. Don't fall for the enemy's tricks and lies! Be alert and be on guard as a soldier. Soon it will become a routine if you choose to go the way of the sinners. You'll start listening to their ungodly advice because they will appear to have it all together. Their counsel will persuade you to the point that soon you will be walking with them and listening to their advice. Soon you will begin sitting with them and hanging out with them. Sitting here means more than just sitting—you are doing what they are doing, getting too comfortable. If this leads to getting high again, you are in deep trouble!

Before you know, it you'll be sitting with the scorners, those who mock God and the things of God. You may even find yourself becoming judgmental and critical like them. You will become labeled as one of them, even if you are not, just because you are with them. And you will start pulling away from God's people and church.

What triggered this? You did, by not staying on God's path no matter what the cost! No matter if it was boring. No matter if it was hard. You can't leave God's ways; you cannot give in and quit because you are lonely or get weary in well doing. Verse 2 says that you are blessed and happy if you are delighting in the Word of God. When you become discontent, you can get off track. You have to make a quality decision to delight in God's ways. You must be with His people in a church where you will be taught the Word of God and they allow the Holy Spirit to move. You must meditate on His Word day and night. Then you will become like a tree that is described in verse 3—a tree that is planted, rooted and established. Being around God's people and in His Word is like living alongside a river of fresh water. You are only going to grow stronger every day and you will produce good fruit and succeed and prosper in whatever you do.

Notice what happens in verses 4-6 to those who don't stay on God's path. Rejoice that you didn't fall for it! Choose the right path and stay on it no matter what, because it will mean life or death to you. It is your life so you must choose life (Deuteronomy 30:19).

Confession

Today, I choose life and not death. I am blessed because I refuse to go down the pathway of sinners. I refuse to listen to those who don't know God, love God or are not living for Him. I asked Jesus to be my Savior and my Lord. I am blessed because I delight myself in His Word and I mediate in it. I think about it all the time. I speak it. I listen to it all day long. I stay far from anything that would get me off of God's path. His words lead me and guide me. I hang around His people. I love to be in the house of the Lord. I am like a tree that is planted by the rivers of water. I am growing stronger every day in whatever I do. I prosper and I have great success. I bear fruit and people see God at work in me. My life shines for Christ. Amen.

Day #6: Read Isaiah 45:2- 7. Notice that it says the crooked places will be made straight. This means that you won't stumble along in the dark like you did when you were not living for God. God is with you now, and

He is holding you up by His right hand of righteousness. God will cause your impossible situations to become possible. You are free and delivered from all addictions and from all the power of the enemy, and nothing shall by any means harm you again. When God is for you, who or what can be against you and succeed? Nothing! He guided you and held you up even before you knew Him. How much more now will He take care of you because you call on His name?

Read and write out Colossians 2: 6-7. _____

_____

_____

_____

_____

_____

_____

_____

_____

_____

_____

_____

_____

Confession

I am planted, rooted and grounded in Christ Jesus. I am firmly planted in His root system. I am built up in Him and established in the faith. I am very thankful and grateful for all that Christ has done for me. He has set me free from a life of instability and defeat. He has delivered me from deception; I now have a sound and sober mind. I know what the will of the Lord is for me and that is to stay clean, so I do! And I will rejoice in that truth. I confess whom the Son Jesus has set free is free indeed. I am free indeed! I am blessed, and my heart is at rest. I face life one day at a time, one breath at a time. Amen.

Use a dictionary to define the following words:

delivered _____

_____

_____

established _____

_____

_____

grounded _____

_____

_____

rooted _____

_____

_____

purposed _____

_____

_____

This is what God has done for you and is continuing to do in you as you do the Word and not just hear it. When the Word of God gets down deep inside of your soul and heart and you know that you are delivered, then you will become established—grounded and rooted in

Him. Then you will be able to pursue and fulfill your purpose.

Day #7: Read John 15 and choose a favorite scripture to meditate on. Write it out here: _____

_____

_____

_____

_____

_____

_____

Verse 7 says, "If ye abide in me and my words abide in you, you shall ask what you will and it will be done for you." John 15 says that Jesus is the vine and we are connected to Him. We are the branches. He is our life source. Verse 5 says, "And without me you can do nothing." We must make this our daily confession because we cannot truly stay sober, we cannot stay out of sin, and we cannot do anything worth anything, without Him living in and through us. We are dependent on Him. Praise God, we are no longer controlled by this world's addictions! We now get high on the Most High, our Lord Jesus Christ!

Read 1 John 3:16-24 and write out what these verses mean to you. _____

_____

_____

_____

_____

_____

_____

_____

_____

_____

_____

_____

_____

_____

_____

_____

_____

Confession

As He is, so am I in this present world. I am a doer of the Word of God and not just a hearer only. I am not deceived. I know He loved me and laid down His life for me, so I also lay down my life and my desires, and I put Him first place in my life.

I abide in Him and He abides in me. I am not condemned. When I mess up, I fess up and I get up! I get right immediately for I know He loves me, forgives me and does not condemn me. Therefore, I am free from all condemnation and I will not condemn myself. His Holy Spirit lives in me and helps me, teaching me what is right and what is not right. I hear His voice and I do follow. I am not tossed to and fro anymore; I am established in Him. He is my life now. The former things have passed away; they died when I died. Now I am alive forevermore in Him. He is the vine and I am the branch. My life source is plugged into His life. I live because He lives. My life has forever been transformed—and all because of Christ Jesus, my Lord!

NOTES

_____

_____

_____

_____

_____

_____

_____

_____

_____

_____

_____

_____

_____

_____

_____

_____

_____

_____

_____

_____

_____

_____

MILESTONE #8 LOOKING INTO THE MIRROR — WHO I AM IN CHRIST

The eighth milestone is that I need divine intervention. I need to see myself the way Christ sees me in Him. When I can see myself as He sees me, I will know my future and purpose. I look into the mirror of God's Word so I can see myself as He sees me—in Christ. I am not the person I used to be; old things have passed away and all things have become new in my life. I am no longer deceived. I can see clearly now. I know who I am; all fear is gone. Jesus has come to live inside of me. I am not the same; my life is changed. I am in Him and He is in me.

The life that I now live, I live by the faith of the Son of God, who loved me and gave Himself for me. I have been bought with a price, the blood of Christ. I belong to God. My life is hid in Christ. As He is, so am I in this world. He has given me skills and gifts to use for His will and good pleasure. My life is a beacon that shines bright so others may see Jesus in me. I will not hide my light under a bushel; I will let it shine bright for others to see so they may come to the light. Jesus is the light of the world, and everyone who receives Him, receives light to see, just as I now see. I know who I am in Christ Jesus and I have the victory! Amen.

Day #1: Today is the beginning of the rest of my life! I

will not leave here like I came, in Jesus' name. I have made a decision to change, and God will help me. I am not alone. God's people will help me. And most of all I will help myself! Because I am free, I intend to stay free! Amen.

The Word of God is the Mirror of Truth (James 1:22-25).

We look into a mirror to see what we look like. It is said that when one looks into a mirror, it will never lie. The reflection you see is the real you. Every wrinkle, gray hair, and bulge will show. You can't hide from the truth! Well, the Bible, God's Word, is said to be a mirror. It is the mirror of truth. You can look into it and see who you are naturally and spiritually. Sometimes people don't like what they see because it reminds them of their shortcomings. But it will also show them how to change. God wants you to look into His Word so you can find out who you are and start enjoying His life.

The Bible is your life's manual. It will give wisdom, provide guidance, and show you where you are missing it or when you're doing right. It will tell you who you are now in Christ. It will show you your future. It will show you that you are righteous now. All of mankind's answers are in the Word of God, if people would just take time to seek them out. We have the power to overcome addictions because of righteousness.

Righteousness means _____

_____

_____

_____

We have the power because God has given us authority in His name. That name has all power and every knee must bow to the name _____ . We can call on His name in prayer. That is our right as a child of God. We have power through what we confess. Romans 10:9-10 says we believe in our heart and we speak with our mouth. What I believe, I speak and I do. I am a doer of the Word of God. My words are my life! His Words are my life. I mediate on them day and night. I am like a tree that is by the rivers of water: growing strong and rooted and established in Him. I will not be moved when troubles come my way because I know they will pass, and I will endure and last through Christ Jesus my Lord.

I am a brand new person. I am free from the past (2 Corinthians 5:14-21). Righteousness and restoration are fellowshipping with God on legal ground because of what Jesus' blood did for us. Jesus did what we could not do; He made a way for us to have fellowship with the Father. His work was enough to restore us to God. We are now in relationship with God. I was once without God and without hope, but now I have hope. I know things are changing in my life because I desire them to change and I am doing something about it! All things that the enemy has stolen have been restored to me, so I go and possess them. Hallelujah!

Jeremiah 29:11 says that God has given me a

_____ and _____.

We have God's Nature in us now. I have the power to overcome addictions because of His righteousness. We are in right standing with God. No matter where we are at in our walk with God, we have the ability to stand in His presence and expect to receive answers. The devil, his demons, nor any situation can stop us! We can stand boldly in His throne room without the sense of guilt, sin consciousness, inferiority, or condemnation. We are masters over sin because of Christ.

Look into the perfect law of liberty—God's Word. Look into the mirror and see what God sees in you. Say, "In Jesus' name, I am delivered." Use the name of Jesus and tell the enemy where to go! A great exchange took place when you got born again. God's Life came into you. You have been redeemed. Redemption means you were removed from _____ and

_____ . You were delivered from all _____ and its consequences.

Day #2: Read 1 John 1:1-10. He is light and in Him is no _____. We are lying if we say we have fellowship with Him but continue to live in darkness. Write verse 7: _____

_____

_____

_____

_____

When we mess up, we can count on it that Jesus will _____

_____.

When we ask forgiveness, we can start over. God is always faithful and _____ to get us back in right standing with Him. If we say we have not sinned then we what? _____

So admit it and get rid of it. Receive your forgiveness. Don't let it steal your joy. God is a fair and just Father, just like you are to your own kids! You want them to fess up and get on with the day, right?

That is how God wants you to be, like a child—His child. Our motto and the Milestone motto to live by is "When I mess up, I fess up, and then I get up!"

You no longer live in darkness like you did before. Ephesians 2:2-6 says, "Wherein times past, you walked according to the course of this world, according to the prince of the power of the air, the spirit that now worketh in the children of disobedience." You were once a child of disobedience but now you are a child of God. Verses 5-6 says we were dead in our sins, but now we are alive unto God and He hath raised us up together and made us sit together in heavenly places in Christ Jesus. In other words, as He is so am I. Verse 12 says that I was without Christ, an alien from the commonwealth of Israel and stranger from the covenants of promise, having no hope and without God in the world. But now in Christ Jesus, ye who were sometimes far off are made near by the blood of Jesus. You see we did not have God in our lives, neither did we know Him, but He knew us! We were aliens from the children of God, and aliens from the promises of God.

Go through the book of Ephesians and highlight every time you see the words "in Him" or "in Christ." Write out at least four of these verses.

_____

_____

_____

_____

_____

_____

_____

_____

_____

_____

_____

_____

_____

Ephesians 1:18 says the _____ of our _____
are enlightened and we can see clearly now who we are, and we can
clearly see His will for our lives. This is seeing spiritually or having
spiritual discernment to know what is right and what is not right so
we can make good choices.

Write out and confess Psalm 27:1.

_____

_____

_____

_____

Confession

You, O Lord are my light and my salvation. I was blind, but now
I see clearly. I am no longer deceived. Your ways are the right way,
O Lord. Your Word is a lamp unto my feet and a light unto my path.
No longer will I stumble around in the darkness. I know my future.
You are my future, and my future is bright. The eyes of my inner man
have been opened. I know Your will, I hear Your voice, and I see Your
path for my life, and that will I follow. Today is the day that You have
made and I will rejoice and be glad in it, for I am in Christ. Amen.

Day #3: Read Colossians 3:1- 6. Verse 1 says, "If ye then be risen with Christ, seek those things that are above, where Christ sits on the right hand of God. Set your _____on things and not on things of the _____. For ye are dead and your life is hid with Christ in God." Write out what this means to you: ___

_____

_____

_____

_____

_____

_____

_____

We have been saying over and over that we are new creatures in Christ and the old person that we used to be is dead. So what happened to our old man? Well, when Christ died, went to hell, conquered Satan, and then arose from the dead, to be seated at the right hand of Father God, He did it all for us. He conquered and defeated the enemy, even death. Now we will never have to experience or see hell, that is, if we are born again.

We were dead in ourselves and destined for hell because of what Adam did. But Jesus, the second Adam, came that we might have life and live it more abundantly. When we believe and receive that revelation into our lives, our spirit man is made alive unto Him. We literally died that day when we asked Jesus into our lives. Then we became reborn —born again. Things have changed! Our outlook on life has taken a 180 degree turnaround. We are now alive and can see clearly. The scales have been removed from our eyes. People are amazed by our change.

If you had been out of fellowship with God but now are restored, then it is the same in your life. You are brand new and back on track. No matter how long it has been, ten hours or ten years, how wonderful it is to have another chance in life. Every day is a new day—a brand new start! Now you must set your affections (emotions, desires, thoughts and will) upon Him and not on this world (Colossians 3:1-2).

That doesn't mean that you have to become fanatical and weird, but you do have restraints and should do things differently now. The living God is living on the inside of you, and your desires have totally changed. You are dead and alive unto God!

When you live for God, you will soon discover you need to be around His people. That means the old "friends" will start disappearing. As you talk about the Lord, they won't stick around. But this is your life now. Second Corinthians 6 asks how can darkness and light fellowship together. They can't! So not only do you change from the inside out, but the outside begins to change as well. That means that if you had problems with certain hang- ups or addictions, you will soon realize you don't want those things anymore and they will fall by the wayside. Now that is transformation! When you change from the inside out, that is when your life really changes. Ask God to help you to grow up "in Christ" and be all you were meant to be.

Confession

Father, I now realize that I am changed through the blood of Your Son Jesus Christ. My life has been transformed. I have been changed. I know that it was all a gift from You. Even the faith to believe was from You. You pulled me up out of the darkness and gave me light.

Please help me to live for You, to serve You with all my heart, soul and body. I know the flesh, the outer man, is weak, but I am strong in You. I can do all things because You are helping me, and You live on the inside of me. Thank You, Lord, for this new life and the chance to start all over again. Thank You, Lord, for forgiving me. Amen.

Read and write out 1 John 4:4.

_____

_____

_____

_____

Day #4: Write out Ephesians 2:8-10.

_____

_____

_____

_____

_____

_____

_____

_____

Confession

I have been ordained and destined to walk in good works. God has a plan for my life. I will not waste time anymore. And I will not live in a self-destruct mode. I am a new person and the old man and the old ways no longer exist in my life. I live life to the fullest now! I am the handiwork of God. He has special plans for me. I have a hope and a future. I am unique and have gifts and talents designed just for me and the calling on my life.

Not one person is like me. I have my own set of fingerprints. I even have my own voiceprint! My voice is unique unto the Lord. He hears me when I cry unto Him. He hears me when I sing praises to His name. I will praise Him with all that is within me, bless His Holy name (Psalm 103:1, Psalm 40:1).

I have been destined to praise the Lord and my hands have been anointed to do His plan for my life. No more wasted years for me! This is the day that the Lord has made and I will rejoice and be glad in it. Hallelujah!

God made us all unique and gave us certain gifts and talents. People are not nurses, soldiers, or teachers by accident. It is an innate desire that draws people to certain interests and occupations. We all have our calling to fulfill. It comes naturally when it is your gift! Sometimes people inherit a job by default——it was passed down to them and they may feel that there is no way out. Search your heart and ask yourself what you like to do. Ask God to show you what He wants you to do, too. I used to be afraid that I was going to end up in Africa and live in a hut if I asked God what He wanted me to do, but then I learned if it isn't in my heart, it isn't going to happen! God literally gives us the desire to do what He wants us to do. If you desire it, then most likely it is your calling. Pursue it!

Whether you are just starting your life out as an adult or starting all over, it is never too late to do His will for your life. It pays to obey and you will be abundantly satisfied. Ask yourself what you are good at doing, what are your interests and desires. What prospers every time you do it? What do you have favor in doing? What do you like to do?

Write out at least four things you are good at doing.

_____

_____

_____

_____

_____

_____

_____

_____

_____

_____

Jeremiah 1:5 says that you are fearfully and wonderfully made. God knew you before you were ever born when you were still in your mother's womb. He knows every hair on your head. He knows everything about you, every detail. That is who He is! He is our creator.

Day #5: Isaiah 43:18-19 says, "Remember ye not the former things, neither consider the things of old. Behold, I will do a new thing; now it shall spring forth; shall ye not know it? I will even make a way in the wilderness, and rivers in the desert."

God says stop looking back at the past. You can't do anything about it anyway. It is history! It's gone forever! Start looking forward to the new things in your life. The new way of doing things, the new people, and the new future that now awaits you. The past is gone; it cannot be changed. But your future is before you—whatever you want it to be!

Choose Christ and you will choose the good life. This is your focus now. Leave the past behind or you will never move forward. You are in Christ and He is in you. The sky is the limit now! Dare to believe it! No situation is impossible for God. It may be impossible with men, but not with God. It might be impossible for you, but it is not impossible with God inside of you. Think "God inside-minded."

In your heart, you know God is doing a new work in you. Allow it to take root. Grow in Him. Mature in Christ. Don't be like little children, up and down emotionally or tossed to and fro as it says in Ephesians 3:17. We are no longer tossed to and fro. We are rooted and established in Him! Don't allow the devil or others tell you things will never change. Tell yourself, they have already changed, because you have made a decision to change.

If the enemy tells you something isn't going to happen, you can be guaranteed it is going to happen! Satan is a liar; he never tells the truth. God's promises in His Word are true and they are always 'Yes' and 'Amen.'

So be it in my life! Your will, Father God – so be it in my life! I live this life for You now. I am not my own; I have been bought with a price—the blood of the Lord Jesus Christ. I have been crucified with Christ. I am now alive unto God and He lives and moves and has His way in me. All His promises are 'Yes' and 'Amen' for me. I believe it and I receive it! Hallelujah!

Read Joshua 1. Moses was dead and Joshua had to make a

decision to go forward. He was given the task of to taking the children of Israel into the Promised Land. He probably felt overwhelmed in the natural since he was responsible for over a million people or so. Without God's direction and supernatural assistance, he couldn't have done it. But he did it, and you can make it, too! God will help you. Write out Joshua 1:5-6:

Confession

As God was with Moses and Joshua, so He is with me. No man, no power, no demon—can stand in my way of doing God's will for my life. I submit myself to God and resist the devil and he flees from me in terror. He knows that I know my authority and he will not stick around. I know that my Father God loves me. He will never leave me or forsake me. He will not abandon me as others may have done in the past. I am strong and of good courage as I press on.

God will make a way where there seems to be no way. I dare to believe and trust in Him. I am not afraid to go forward. My future is bright in Christ. My Father holds me in the palm of His hand so I am not alone. He is with me wherever I go! Wherever He sends me, there will I go—and I will prosper as I obey Him. Amen.

Day #6: Read Romans 6:1-2. We no longer want to continue living in sin. We have been set free from sin. Verses 4-6 say that our old man is crucified with Christ. Our sins were nailed to the cross with Him. He who knew no sin became sin for us so we could become like Him—the righteousness of God in Him. Meditate on these verses and write out what the Lord reveals to you about who you are now. _____

_____

_____

_____

Romans 6:14 says, "For sin shall not have dominion over you: for ye are not under the law, but under grace." Verse 17-18 says, "Ye were the servants of sin, but ye have obeyed from the heart that form of doctrine which was delivered you. Being then made free from sin, ye became the servants of righteousness." Verse 22 says, "But now being made free from sin, and become servants to God, ye have your fruit unto holiness, and the end everlasting life."

When I was set free, I became a servant of righteousness and now I have a productive life in Christ. I am free from the old man and his bad habits and addictions. I am a new creation in Christ Jesus and old things are passed away forever! Amen.

Confession

My life is not my own, I have been bought with a price, the blood of Jesus Christ. I have been crucified with Him, and most of all I have been raised with Him. I have His nature in me now and I do not want to sin. I hate sin and flee from it—and it flees from me! Sin doesn't dominate me anymore. I have been set free and I am alive unto God for His glory. Amen.

Day #7: Write out Romans 6:23.

_____

_____

_____

_____

It actually takes work to sin and go our own way, especially after we have become children of God. Our spirit man doesn't want to go against God. However, our flesh will always give in and rebel against holiness. God gives us a free gift that leads to life. But the way of sin leads to death. The word "wages' is used in Romans 6:23, but you don't receive a paycheck. Instead, you have to pay out! Think about that! Sin never gives you anything, but it will always cost you something. And many times, it costs a lot more than just money! What fool in his mind would work so hard to die or to destroy himself? That is what a person does who is caught up in addictions. He is killing himself! It might be a slow suicide, but nevertheless, it does lead to death.

All of my old party buddies are either incarcerated, dead or wish they were dead. Nothing good comes out of addictions. Addictions take away everything so dear and precious to us. This is one of

Satan's most effective tactics to destroy mankind.

Read Romans 8 and carefully reread it over and over again. Choose scriptures that speak to you and write them down. This is God speaking to us! The number one way that you will hear God's voice is through His Word, because He and His Word are one.

Write out Romans 8:1 and memorize this scripture. _____

_____

_____

_____

You will probably need to remind yourself of this scripture every day so you will not feel condemned when things don't go right. Sometimes they won't always go right, but you must put on the attitude of "I will not give up, I will not quit!" Then get back up and start over and boldly declare this scripture.

Read Romans 8:11-16 and write out what these scriptures mean to you.

_____

_____

_____

_____

_____

_____

_____

_____

Confession

I am not condemned. Jesus has set me free. His Word tells me that I am free from condemnation. Therefore, I believe it and receive it. I have not received the spirit of fear, but I have received the spirit of Christ. I have the spirit of God inside of me and I cry 'Abba Father.' God is my Heavenly Father and I am His child. He loves me and gave His all for me. I am more than a conqueror because of His love for me. Praise the Lord!

NOTES

_____

_____

_____

_____

_____

_____

_____

_____

_____

_____

_____

_____

_____

_____

MILESTONE #9 GOODBYE PAST, HELLO FUTURE!

The ninth milestone is that I need divine intervention to let go of the past once and for all. It's behind me so I must stop bringing it to my present. It's time to go forward and stop looking back.

There is a saying, "If you keeping looking back, then pretty soon, you'll be back." Someone once told me that it is impolite to talk about the dead. That is how it is when you keep talking about your past. It is dead. That person doesn't exist anymore. So bury your past; let it go and move on! You are not the only one who has gone through stuff. Everyone has experienced some sort of crisis, loss or hardship. But you must not get stuck in a cycle of grief over it. You must get up and press on to your future, to what lies ahead for you in Christ Jesus. He is your life now. Let the dead bury the dead, while you start living!

> Day #1: Today is the beginning of the rest of my life! I will not leave here like I came, in Jesus' name. I have made a decision to change and God will help me change. I am not alone. God's people will help me. And most of all I will help myself! Christ has set me free and I intend to stay free at whatever cost. No more bondage for me! Addictions do not have control over me any longer. I have a hope and a future now—and it is in Christ!

In the Recovery Bible, Philippians 3: 13-14 says, "I am still not all I should be, but I am focusing all my energies on this one thing: forgetting the past and looking forward to what lies ahead. I strain to reach the end of the race and receive the prize for which God is calling me up to heaven."

You can't go forward until you let go of what is behind!

The Rearview Mirror Syndrome – You cannot keep looking in the rearview mirror and drive forward, because sooner or later you will crash! All your focus must be on what lies ahead. Alcohol, drugs, pornography or whatever addiction you may have dealt with were all counterfeits for the real deal—God! They kept us stuck in the "past" mode. We couldn't move forward and we could barely function in the present because we were stuck in a time warp. This state of a being wrecked in limbo has kept us in a state of unrest, uncertainty, and most of all, it has kept us trapped in fear. Fear and peace don't mix, as everyone soon discovers.

Fear and peace are opposites that don't attract. Fear brings torment while peace provides rest for the soul. God wants us to have peace more than anything, but unless it is His way, it's not going to happen! His way is to press on to what lies ahead while letting go of what is behind. This is the beginning of true liberty—when we can see there still is a hope and a future for us.

Read Proverbs 14:12 says, "There is a way which seemeth right unto a man, but the end thereof are the ways of death." We drank and did harmful things to our bodies, then became addicted. We couldn't quit! We were snake-bitten! It turned on us as it always does. People also turned on us as they always do in this dysfunctional lifestyle of insanity.

Ask yourself, "Have you had enough yet? Are you ready to get off the roller coaster ride and start living a life on solid ground?" God never turns on us. His peace is not that way. God is not that way! His way is the right way; this world's way and our way lead to death. You've tried everything else. Can't you give God a try?

You must look at addictions now as a life or death situation. If you don't, then it is just a matter of time before you go back to these things. Then you will become worse off than before!

Father God will not leave us. He promises that He will never abandon or forsake us like our "so-called" friends have done, or even our own earthly fathers did. Even if we turned our backs on God and forsake Him, He will never give up on us! In Hebrews 13:5-7, God says, "Let your conversation be without covetousness; and be content with such things as ye have: for He hath said, I will never leave thee, nor forsake thee. So that we may boldly say, The Lord is my helper, and I will not fear what man shall do unto me. Remember them which have the rule over you, who have spoken unto you the word of God: whose faith follow, considering the end of their conversation. In Matthew 7:14, Jesus tells us that there are two roads that we can choose to travel down in life. One road is popular. It's easy and wide, but it leads to self-destruction. The other road is narrow and will be difficult at times, because it is less traveled. However, this narrow path leads to life. Jesus said that He is that way. John 14:6 reads, "I am the way, the truth and the life, no man cometh unto the Father, but by me!"

The Insanity of Addictions

In the Recovery Bible, Proverbs 23:29-35 says, "Who has anguish? Who has sorrow? Who is always fighting? Who is always complaining? Who has unnecessary bruises? Who has bloodshot eyes? It is the one who spends long hours in the taverns, trying out new drinks. Don't let the sparkle and smooth taste of wine deceive you, because in the end, it bites like a poisonous serpent—it stings like a viper. You will see hallucinations and say crazy things. You will stagger like a sailor tossed at sea, clinging to a swaying mast. And you will say, 'They hit me, but I didn't feel it. I didn't even know it when they beat me up. When will I wake up so I can have another drink?'"

We know what drink does, yet we keep going back to it. We get stuck and think we can't get out. It's a cycle of madness with no stability, no purpose, and no future. Or maybe you're just not ready to get out yet. Maybe you need another ten years. It will take much effort on your part to go forward for sure! Or perhaps, you haven't suffered enough yet. But when YOU are ready—God is waiting. He is ready to lead you out and into your Promised Land. He will bring you out with a mighty hand. People will be amazed and say that only God could have done that! He will help you. His people will be waiting to help you, too. You won't have to do it alone.

Of course, the devil will be mad and all hell will probably break loose. He will try to trip you up so you will give up. And if you mess up, he will be ready to hammer away so you will withdraw being so ashamed and condemned. But be alert and ready for his tactics. Remind yourself of who lives in you now; you are not alone to fight this battle—Christ has already won!

Why We Don't Want to Let Go of the Past

- 1. Fear of Being Alone – Your decision to change could mean cutting off long time relationships They may have been unhealthy and fruitless but you may say to yourself, "Well, at least they have always been there for me and I'm not alone." The bond between old school friends or a romance can suck the life out of you! You need to always ask yourself this question when involved in any kind of relationship, "Is this person bringing me closer to God or taking me further away from Him?" This is a gauge to know whether it is a safe relationship or not.

I realize that we can't change our family, but we may have to create distance between some of our family members. Besides, your walk is between you and God—and no one else! So you have to do what it takes to stay clean and sober and the only true way that you will be able to do this is by living in Christ. There is no other way! You may have to separate from some folks to be able to see life clearly, instead of from their perspective.

I have learned that when you tell people about your "issues," they always think they have to offer advice. If you tell twenty people something, you will get twenty opinions. This can create a lot of confusion. It is important to only share intimate details about your life with just a few "safe" people who will help you in your recovery process. Also, what may be a secret to you may not be so precious and kept secret by others. Don't tell everything to everyone! If you do, some may start avoiding you like you have a disease or something! Always ask yourself before you start talking and telling someone everything, "What is their need to know this information about me?" (We will learn more of this in Milestone #11 Friend vs. Foe.)

> • 2. Fear of Change and the Unknown – You're in your comfort zone and at least you have some control and are familiar with it – even if it is dysfunctional! The children of Israel were whining in the wilderness to go back to Egypt, even though they knew it was detrimental for them. "At least we were taken care and had food and shelter," they told themselves. This would be similar to you saying, "At

least someone loved me and made me feel special, even if it was an abnormal relationship. At least I felt good and wasn't alone. At least they didn't fail me like my own family did." The excuses go on and on!

The Israelites seemed to forget how they cried day and night, year after year, for a way out—for God to deliver them. Then when He did deliver them, they were afraid to go forward. They were afraid of change. They were afraid of being uncomfortable in unfamiliar surroundings. And most of all, they were afraid of the unknown, of starting all over. I've seen this happen a lot with older people. When they should be going forward, they retreat and pull back in fear. As a result, they continue stuck in the same old cycle until the next time around, if there ever even is that chance again. For some, there won't be that next time!

In Hebrews, God says He is not pleased with the man of God who pulls back. The children of Israel were consumed with fear, doubt, unbelief, so that was all they could speak. They ended up dying—not in Egypt and not in the Promised Land—but stuck in the desert, in their own valley of indecision! They were children of God who pulled back in their believing. It would have been better to make some decisions and fail than to die and never try anything.

Why do you want to play it safe in an unsafe world with unsafe people? Do you really think you are safe? To me, this is pure stupidity! God brings you out of the pit, He delivers you from drugs, a homosexual lifestyle or whatever your addiction was, and what are you going to do with it? Go back? God forbid! But if you do mess up, just fess up and get back up! Get up and get out of there as quick as you can! Run like Joseph did. If you don't, then it will be like crucifying the Lord all over again! It's like saying that what He did for you wasn't enough.

You may say, "It won't work for me; my situation is different. I have these special problems. I was abused. I was taken advantage of. My parents died when I was young. I was abandoned and was forced to live on the streets." The excuses go on and on! What you are doing is giving into the flesh, your unrenewed thoughts and most of all, the devil. He is there patting you on the back, telling you it is okay to be depressed, after all, you have been through so much. These are the same thoughts that got you into an addictive lifestyle in the first place! If you keep fueling and feeding the flesh and don't replace your thoughts with His thoughts, you will end up worse than before! Luke 11:24-25 tells us this. All of us have gone through some unpleasant circumstances in life, but the key is "gone through." We didn't get stuck! You can't allow yourself to get stuck because it will destroy everything if you do!

- 3. Fear of Failure – There are people who have messed up so much that they don't know if they can ever succeed in anything again, so they quit before they even get started. This usually stems from low self-esteem. Perhaps they were emotionally and verbally abused to the point that they second guess everything they do, therefore sabotaging their own success. They will rarely succeed in anything with this mindset.

In my early Christian years, after I got hired for a job, I would go back to the boss to make sure he really knew all the "dirt" on me (I was a convicted felon) to see if he still wanted me. I felt so worthless and at that time, couldn't understand how anyone could see any good in me. I did this over and over again until I got tired of losing jobs, and a wise sister in the Lord told me that I didn't need to tell so much information.

She also advised me to always ask myself this question

before I even opened my mouth: "What is their need to know this information?" I learned I couldn't trust just anyone and needed to use discretion. In fact, I still pray daily for discretion so I will be wise in all of my affairs. I ask the Lord to help me to see myself as He sees me with an "I can do mentality." The truth is, if you don't think you can, then you can't. As a man thinks in his heart, so is he! One cannot do what he does not believe he can do.

Another example of this was when I once asked my rich uncle if I could take his brand new Cadillac for a drive. I made the mistake of taking him, my brother, my son and my husband for a ride with me. They made fun of me and made me so nervous that I literally ran off the road and almost killed us all! Their negative words affected me so much that I couldn't function. I actually thought I couldn't drive, even though I had been driving for years! Of course, I knew they were just kidding when they were making fun of me in the car, yet I had internalized all of the negative words that I heard all of my life to the point that I failed and couldn't even do a simple task at like drive a car!

Philippians 4:8 says, "Finally, brethren, whatsoever things are true, whatsoever things are honest, whatsoever things are just, whatsoever things are pure, whatsoever things are lovely, whatsoever things are of good report; if there be any virtue, and if there be any praise, think on these things." It is so important to replace our thoughts with God's thoughts and mediate on good things. Then when we hear negative words, they will bounce off of us because our minds will be so renewed to the truth! These words will have little impact on us and we won't internalize them. Otherwise, negative words truly can make or break our self-esteem.

You have heard the saying: Sticks and stones may break my bones, but words will never hurt me. Well, that is a lie! The body will heal from the sticks and stones, but those negative words go deep down into the soul and can ruin a person's life. Those words can linger for many years and cause a lot of damage to a person's way of thinking, if they are even able to recover from them at all!

• 4. Fear of Responsibility – Some people don't want to carry their own load, let alone someone else's. This is a self-centered mentality because one is only concerned about himself. For example, look at a homeless person. (I say this from experience because I was homeless at one time.) Now, I know not every homeless person is this way, but there are more that are, than are not! They become wanderers and drifters, not productive in society. They live for the next fix and are always on a street corner waiting for a hand-out, which is their spending money because the government has already provided them with free shelter, food, and bus transportation. Their families usually don't know where they are because they disappear and don't want to be found.

God wants more than this from us. He wants us to contribute to society with our knowledge, our labor, and most of all, our life, so we can be a witness for Him. If we are beggars, we are not glorifying God with our lives. If we are users of people, we are not glorifying God. If we are shut-ins and don't work, we are not glorifying the Lord. If we abandon our responsibilities in life, we are definitely not bringing glory to God. Besides, we have people waiting for us in our realm of influence to get our act together so we can reach them for Christ. What we do, does affect others!

• 5. Fear of Letting Go of "The Good Ole Days" - Very few people grew up with a wonderful childhood, but there are some exceptions. Almost everyone has something they wish they could erase from their past. First, there is the one who had a great childhood but is just not ready to let go of it. He doesn't want to grow up and let go of the relationships or the era of his childhood. He keeps trying to recreate the good old days. This goes along with the fear of change and responsibility. You see people like this who still wear the same clothes from high school, and they're forty years old! They still talk about the good old days and collect memorabilia from their "time." You want to go over and smack them and say, "Grow up!"

The second one has good memories, but maybe something beyond their control happened to abruptly change all that and turn their happy world inside out such as a car wreck, abduction, divorce, or molestation. They haven't been able to move forward because they won't let go of the bad memories. Therefore, they consume him and causes him to be stuck.

Some people try to keep things the same (denial) to keep those "good ole memories" alive, while suppressing the negative ones. I have seen some even set up a shrine in memory of the lost loved one by leaving a room the same and making it like a museum. They refuse to go forward. This affects their future, and everyone else around them is tarnished by it.

For example, a divorce occurs and the family pretends like everything is okay so the neighbors won't think differently or the children, (if they are young enough, won't know what is going on. This façade lives on because they feel like it is very important that everything and everyone continue to appear normal and happy to outsiders. I have seen this in ministers' homes, and then their kids turn out wild and everyone is scratching their heads wondering why!

I remember when I turned eleven years old and discovered that my stepdad wasn't my real father. He didn't even live with us, even though he came home every day for dinner and hung out with the family, tucked us in bed each night, and made sure we prayed his catholic prayers. What a shock it was to discover that he went home to Grandma's house every night to sleep, because he and my mom had been separated for many years!

My real dad was in prison. It seemed like I had blocked out memories of him because they were detrimental for me to remember and they all occurred before I was four years old anyway. At the time, my brother was six years old so he remembers more than I do. But then the violent flashbacks started haunting me—the FBI, the mob, the betrayal, the fear, the abandonment, the lies, and my mom's nonstop nightly drunks. Her sobbing kept replaying in my head. These things shattered my world and I lost all trust in my parents. All the good memories of the past with my "daddy" were being replaced with the bad dreams of my real father slicing my mom with a knife and the mob taking all of our furniture because of his gambling debts. All of these dormant memories began to take precedence in my mind. Drinking and drugging seemed to be a good way for me to silence those memories— so that is just what I did!

It is time to say goodbye to all the good, the bad, and the ugly! Besides, it is the past and I want to go forward! I can't stay camped there. I must shake it off and let it go once and for all. I don't want to pay anyone back any more! I release them and let go and I allow my loving Heavenly Father to heal me now and remove all the painful memories of the past. I denounce you Satan and all your demons that I invited in unknowingly because of staying in self-pity and depression. Be gone from me now! Leave me now in Jesus' name. I am allowing You, my Heavenly Father, to close the doors that I had opened to the enemy and to heal me once and for all. Take away all the pain the hurts in Jesus' name. I render them ineffective against me now in Jesus' name. I forgive all those who harmed me and did not care for me as they should have. I let it all go now in the mighty name of Jesus!

Confession

I am pressing on to what lies ahead and I am going to stop looking back. The past is behind me now; it is history! I can't change it so I make a conscious effort to forget it and move on. I move forward to the prize God has for me in Christ Jesus. I am ready for a change. I will not fear the future, because God is my future. My life is in His hands.

I have made Jesus my Lord and I release all rights to controlling my life from this day forward. I will trust in the Lord and lean not on my own understanding. I have tried my way, now I will do God's way. God's path leads to life so I leave death behind me and press on. I may not know every detail about my future, but I trust God to lead me and guide me. I take it one day at a time. In Jesus' name, I pray. Amen.

Day #2: Write out John 14:1, 18, 27._____

_____

_____

_____

_____

_____

_____

_____

_____

_____

_____

_____

_____

_____

_____

_____

_____

_____

_____

_____

_____

_____

_____

We were looking for peace in all the wrong places. We thought we could get it from the booze and drugs. We put on the attitude of "after all, I deserve to feel good." So we got high but in the end, it almost destroyed everything that was so dear to us, including our very lives! But now I know what true peace is—it comes from God. Even in the midst of a storm or crisis, I can be at rest. I will not fear anymore or be anxious about anything. I can be at rest no matter what is going on around me. Christ is in me, and He stabilizes me. He is the anchor of my soul. Read Psalm 23 and write out what this psalm means to you.

_____

_____

_____

_____

_____

_____

_____

_____

What are ways you seek to get peace and rest?

_____

_____

_____

_____

Does it work? If not, what changes should you make? _____

_____

_____

Day #3: Read Numbers 11 about the children of Israel and how they began to complain. They were afraid of the unknown—afraid of change. They were afraid of not having a controlled environment, even if it was dysfunctional! They missed the bread and fish in Egypt. They forgot about the beatings, the slavery, and the heavy burdens. Their complaining displeased the Lord.

We must watch our hearts and not forget how God brought us out of difficult or impossible situations. It might take time for things to settle down, it is a big change to leave one way of life for another. But God promises His way is life! He desires to give us the land with milk and honey, the good life. But it will take time. It takes work on our part and most of all, it takes us not giving up because when we do we have to go back to "start" and go around one more time.

Don't quit! Don't give up and say, "It's too hard being out in this desert all alone." God is with you so you will make it to the other side. Remember the other side is Jordan, the Promised Land. Your promised land that God has for you is where you will find true peace, joy and satisfaction in a life worth living. This is where your dreams do come true!

When we were using and living in our dysfunctional life, it was easy to give in. It seemed like it was easier to quit or run away. I know this because I was the biggest runner! When things got too hard or I didn't know how to fix it, I ran from it and never looked back. But running away will never help us mature and learn how to deal with difficult situations. A wise person once told me, "Never burn your bridges with people, because some day you may have to cross over those bridges again." How true that is!

It was heartbreaking for me to cut off a lot of wonderful people from my life. I hurt them so deeply that to this day, they will never get close to me or lift a finger to help me. There were so many times that I took advantage of people's kindness and milked it until there was nothing left for that person to give me. Then I threw that relationship away, because it was no longer beneficial to me. How wrong I was! How selfish and unsafe I was! I broke many hearts instead of being grateful and thankful for them showing me God's goodness and kindness.

Forgive me Lord for living a life to please myself and feed my addictions. Thank You for opening my eyes and setting me free from this destructive lifestyle. Thank You for forgiving me, and from this moment on, I will live to give and not to take from others. I am learning how to value myself and my relationships.

List four things God has done for you (and thank Him):_____

_____
_____
_____
_____
_____
_____
_____

Read Hebrews 3. This chapter talks about the Israelites entering into God's rest. Verse 13 says to encourage each other daily so that our hearts do not become hardened. Verses 15-19 say that many did not enter into the Promised Land, but instead died in the wilderness because of their unbelief and resentment.

In recovery, it is vital to protect your heart from getting hardened. A few ways to do this are: be quick to repent, quick to forgive, and constantly sing praises to the Lord. This will keep your heart pliable and tender (Proverbs 4:23).

A merry heart doeth good like medicine! Read a psalm daily. David wrote most of the psalms and they displayed a full range of emotions. I am sure you can find yourself in one of the psalms. Notice how David may have started out saying the wrong thing, but he always ended up praising God. It is okay to let it all out to your

Heavenly Father; He knows it all anyway! But once you do this, turn it into a time of thanksgiving and praise. David did this over and over again. That's probably why God said David was a man after His own heart.

It is important to not have a meltdown or outburst that you will regret later. Pull away, retreat, and do whatever it takes to not speak during those times, unless it is to sing praise the Lord, of course. Otherwise, it will be hard to take back the words, and the damage will already be done. Our loved ones may forgive us over and over again, but it will get really old if they don't see some sign of hope in our recovery. And we don't know what will be the breaking point—when they will stop being there for us. Don't push it to find out!

True repentance is a true change of heart. You stay changed, no matter what happens. Don't let the enemy jerk your chain. A dog on a chain can only go so far until he is jerked right back to the same place. Recognize the triggers so you don't fall for them over and over again and keep getting jerked back. Have you ever seen a happy chained up dog? No! Remember where you came from!

Confession

I refuse to allow my heart to become bitter, even when I don't understand everything that is going on around me. I trust God will take care of me and deliver me. And I will not forget to thank Him and be cheerful in all that He has done and is doing in my life. I am thankful! I am grateful! I have been set free from the powers of darkness and delivered from the land of bondage.

Whom Christ has set free is free indeed. I am free indeed. I will not complain and miss the past life of slavery. I will not grumble when things don't change quickly enough for me. I know my future is only getting brighter. It is better than yesterday and will even be better tomorrow. I am not going to worry about the cares of this world. God keeps His Word and takes care of me. (Read Matthew 6:33.)

> Day #4: My path gets brighter and brighter as I go forward in Christ.

Read Proverbs 4:20-27. Fill in the blanks.

I must protect my _____

_____ because out of it flows all the issues of my life. It is

_____ and _____

to all those who find God's Word and hide it in their hearts. I

must put away from me a _____

__. My eyes must look _____ or straight

ahead. I must consider the _____

. For my feet to walk on _____And

God promises me that all my ways will be _____

_____

Confession

To be established means that I am rooted, grounded and stable now. I am placed on the right path and the right track for my life. No more stumbling or being lost for me. I hide His Words in my heart that I will not get off the path and sin against Him or against myself. I choose this day to live for the Lord Jesus Christ. I bind you Satan and your cohorts from my path. I am walking straight ahead in Christ. I will not turn to the right or to the left. I will not stumble this day, in Jesus' name! Amen.

Read a proverb each day. The book of Proverbs was created
to coincide with the calendar. For example, if today is the
13th, then you would read Proverbs 13. Read your chapter of
Proverbs and write out a favorite verse from it to mediate on
today. _____

_____

_____

_____

_____

_____

_____

Day #5: Read Philippians 4:4-20. Write out verse 6.

_____

_____

_____

_____

_____

_____

_____

Anxiety means being full of cares, worry, fear and being much
concerned about one's future and needs. But the Bible says we are
to be anxious for nothing. Instead of fretting and worrying, we are
to trust entirely in our Heavenly Father to provide and take care of
us. The Word of God will fill our minds and our hearts as we learn to
trust in Him. What we put in our minds is very important, because

that is what will come out of our mouths.

Verse 8 says we are to think on things that are what? _____

_____

_____

_____

_____

Always stop when you begin to worry and ask yourself, "Am I thinking on what God says to think on or am I full of the cares of this world, worrying about what I am going to eat, what I am going to wear, and how I am going to pay for it? Matthew 6:9 says to remember what you have learned from the Lord, His people, His Word and the Holy Spirit. Every time we want to worry, we need to stop and remember the Word instead. If God will take care of the birds, He will take care of us too! Don't forget who you are and where you are going!

When you do these things, the God of Peace will come in and flood you with His peace, He will be with you and overtake you. He will help you to flee any situation that is not healthy for you. He will provide a way of escape, as He says in 1 Corinthians 10:13. Matthew 6:11-12 talks about having it all or having nothing. The key is the attitude in both situations. No matter what your circumstances look like, you must learn to be content.

Confession

This will pass. It is temporal. Things will change and get better, because I dare to believe God is taking care of me. He is going to turn all this around as I trust in Him. I can't handle it anyway, so I cast it over on Him to carry the load for me. He will carry this heavy burden.

He said to come unto Him all those who are heavy burdened and He will give us rest. So I come unto Him and receive my rest right now, in Jesus' name. Amen.

Write out Philippians 4:13 and memorize this as one of your daily scriptures. _____

_____

_____

_____

You need to learn and quote Philippians 4:19 often: "But my God shall supply all your need according to his riches in glory by Christ Jesus." God will give you whatever you need. After all, He has it all! He is the Almighty God, the creator of heaven and earth. He made it all!

Confession

My God shall supply my every need through Christ Jesus. I have no lack because God has no lack. He is my Father and I am His child. He takes care of me in every situation. I am strong in Him and therefore, I can do all things through Jesus strengthening me. I am ever ready to handle any situation or circumstance that I encounter, because God is in me and is strengthening me. I am content in all things, knowing my God wants the best for me. I will settle for nothing less than His best for my life, from this moment on, in Jesus' name! Amen.

Day #6: Read Acts 9. People were afraid of Paul (Saul) because he was a killer of Christians. People weren't going to believe he had changed so easily. Many weren't sure and couldn't let go of his past so out of fear, they refused to get close to him.

People may feel this way about us, especially loved ones, because they are affected by past experiences with us. We lied to them, robbed them, deceived them, and let them down over and over again. How could they possibly trust in us again? It takes time to convince people that we are changed and different now. And of course, there will still be some who will never ever believe Christ has changed us, because they have been so deeply wounded by our addictions and can't even bear the sight of us now! But that can't stop us from pushing on and living for Christ.

Paul had a dramatic encounter with Jesus on the road to Damascus. (Acts 9) His life was transformed forever. Now, how could he get people to trust that he wouldn't hurt them? Well, it took time. He had to go away for a while to get strong in the Lord. In fact, some say it was fifteen years before anyone ever saw him again. He was a very important Jew who just disappeared. When he first got saved, there were believers who helped him. But, even they had to really hear from God or they could have been afraid of being killed like he had killed so many believers in the past. Was he really changed by Christ? Only time would tell. Only time will tell in your life also.

Remember, some will never believe in you no matter what you do. So move on. They still remember the hurts from the past and they can't let it go. It's as if it is their shield of protection, so they don't get hurt by you ever again. You must understand this. Just stay at a distance to allow healing to occur. All you can do is pray for them and ask God for reconciliation. Begging, nagging, trying to make them jealous, holding money over their head that you owe them, and manipulating will not work! These are works of the flesh (Galatians

5). Move on in your walk in Christ. It may be a lonely walk at times, but remember you are not alone! Jesus is as close as the mention of His name. Say His name over and over when you feel alone: Jesus, Jesus, Jesus.

Read Mark 10:27-31 and write out what these verses mean to you personally.

_____

_____

_____

_____

_____

_____

_____

_____

Day #7: Read Matthew 11:28-30. Write out what these verses mean to you. _____

_____

_____

_____

_____

_____

_____

_____

_____

Write out Proverbs 14:12. _____

_____

_____

_____

_____

_____

_____

_____

_____

Proverbs 16:7 says, "When a man's ways please the Lord, he maketh even his enemies to be at peace with him." How many of us are searching for peace? God wants us to have peace more than we do! He knows how important it is for our souls and relationships. We must get away from strife and anything that robs us of peace. The Bible says to seek peace with all men and pursue it. Chase after it with all your heart and then you will find it. Get away from gossipers and those who indulge in telling on the sins of others. If they will tell you, they will tell on you! They will tell your secrets to others, because they are not faithful people. You cannot afford this!

You have a clean life now, you need to protect it. Don't give the enemy an opportunity to deface you again. Don't throw your pearls before swine, as Jesus said. That means be careful who you confide in, even Christians, because not everyone is going to be for you. So get ready! It is true there really are wolves in sheep's clothing. There are people who say they live for God, yet they are far from Him.

Ask God to help you and to send good healthy friends your way. Pray for a shield of protection around you to keep unclean, seducing spirits and unhealthy people away from you. Find a good church that teaches God's Word and has awesome praise and worship music and most of all, preaches on the importance of being filled with the Holy

Spirit (Jude 20). This is a well-rounded church—a full gospel church!

You need a church to plug into, but also be alert that not everyone there has pure motives —even in church, sad to say! The devil also goes to church. But church is a much healthier place than meeting friends in a bar. Get involved and get used to hanging around healthy people. God will show you who you can trust and who really is interested in your sobriety and well-being.

Confession

Show me thy way O Lord, teach me Thy path. I choose to walk the narrow road with You because I know it leads to life. I want life and not death. I don't run after destructive things anymore. I refuse to go down destructive paths. I separate myself from all uncleanness and unclean people. I pursue things that are good, pure and holy. I choose to live for You now. You are my Lord and there is no other lord over my life now. Addictions don't control me any longer, for I have been set free from a life of sin and death. Jesus is my only life now.

NOTES

_____

_____

_____

_____

_____

_____

_____

_____

_____

_____

_____

_____

_____

_____

_____

_____

MILESTONE #10
SUBSTITUTION THINKING

The tenth milestone is that I need divine intervention to realize the importance of replacing my thoughts with God's thoughts. Then, and only then, will things begin to change in my life. I must first believe things are changed in order for them to change. That's why I don't say that I am an alcoholic or an addict. Instead, I say that I am a new creation in Christ—old things have passed away in my life. All things have been made new now. I am not the person I used to be; I have been transformed and set free!

I know that my thoughts direct my speech and then my actions. Proverbs 23:7 says, "For as he thinketh in his heart, so is he." So I know that my thoughts or my self-talk must line up with His Word; if it doesn't, then it is my responsibility to substitute my thoughts with the Word of God.

Philippians 4:7-8 says to guard your heart and to think on things that are: _____

_____

_____

_____

I have to do it. God won't force me to think on His Word so I have to make a conscious effort to get in the Bible and meditate on His plan for my life. God's Word is His very own DNA on paper! He gave me Himself. Hallelujah!

If I don't get in the Bible and meditate on God's plan for my life, I will not be able to break the cycle of addiction and its strongholds in my mind. God does His part by setting me free, but then I have to do my part to maintain that freedom. He gave me His ability and authority to do so. He would not tell me to do something I could not do. Therefore, I can do all things through Christ who empowers me with strength.

The insanity must end and be put to death! I must stop the insanity in my life by dying daily. I must put down the old desires and habits of the flesh. I know I can't do this on my own, but with the power of God living on the inside me, I can! If I don't change on the inside, I will just be wearing a facade. I will be a phony and no real change will occur. Eventually, the old man will seep through for all to see until he has full reign again and it will be worse than before for me. The Bible says it will be seven times worse! In other words, if I keep talking the same way and doing the same old things, the end result will be the same old thing—destruction and death to all my dreams.

I am not fighting this battle alone. I know that my mind must be transformed. I can't think like before, so I start now by being changed from the inside out, not the outside in. I start right now and ask for divine intervention and I receive it, in Jesus' name. Amen.

Day #1: Today is the beginning of the rest of my life. I will not leave here like I came, in Jesus' name. I have made a decision to change. God will help me! I am not alone. God's people will help me. And most of all, I will help myself because Jesus has set me free and I intend to stay free! Hallelujah!

Read and write what Ephesians 4:22-25 means to you. _____

_____

_____

_____

_____

_____

Think it, talk it, and then you will walk it! This is how we live. Whatever I am thinking on is what I will become. So I must make a conscious effort to think on what I am thinking on, for that is what I will end up speaking and acting out. I believe and therefore, I speak and do!

Read and write out Romans 10:9-10:

_____

_____

_____

_____

_____

_____

_____

_____

Colossians 3:8-10 tells me to put off_____

_____ and to put on _____

Isaiah 55:8-9 says, "For my thoughts are not your thoughts, neither are your ways my ways, saith the Lord. For as the heavens are higher than the earth, so are my ways higher than your ways, and my thoughts than your thoughts." You might say, "Well, of course they are higher than mine." But what is so wonderful is that you can know His ways.

Philippians 3:10 says, "That I may know him, and the power of his resurrection," This has to be such a deep desire of yours and if it is, then things will change in your life. You are on the right path now—God's path.

Proverbs 16:25 says, "There is a way that seemeth right unto a man, but the end thereof are the ways of death." Or we could say it leads to the death of a vision, a path or purpose for that individual's life. Have you ever heard someone say, "I lost my way?" Well, they mean that they have lost their focus of who they are and where they are going. Or perhaps they didn't even know who they were to begin with! If so, they are like many others who are lost and just stumbling through life, hoping things will turn out. But we know it doesn't work that way. Life is not lived by chance. If you are not on God's course for your life, you are on a collision course. It is just a matter of time before you will crash! A good life is from God. Death and destruction come from the enemy (John 10:10). You are traveling on one of these roads and your road will lead to your eternal destiny.

Read Joshua 1:8. What we are to continually do all day long?

_____

_____

_____

In the Recovery Bible Romans 12:1-2 says, "And so dear brother and sisters, I plead with you to give your bodies to God because of all He has done for you. Let them be a living and holy sacrifice – the kind He will find acceptable." This is truly the way to worship God. Don't copy the behavior and customs of this world; let God transform you into a new person by changing the way you think. Then you will learn

God's will for your life.

The Evidence of a New Mind

Write out Hebrews 4:12. _____

_____

_____

_____

_____

_____

_____

The Apostle Paul tells us to avoid being like the world around us. If we copy the behavior and customs of this world, we will imitate its selfish ways and destructive dependencies. Our part is to turn and surrender our lives (spirit, soul, and body) totally over to the care of God. He will help us with our character flaws, but only if we sincerely want that help. As our self-perception (how we see ourselves) changes, our actions will change also. If our self-talk doesn't change, then we will continue acting out addictions because we will still have that same mindset. It is vital that our thoughts change. A mind that hears the Word and does it will be someone who stays clean.

Repentance means _____

_____.

My husband Robert told himself over and over, "I don't want a drink because I don't want to die!" When he saw ads on TV, when he saw his old buddies, when his body was screaming out to him to get high, and when temptation came his way, he dared to say 'no' because he wanted to live and not die. At first, it seemed like many temptations came his way, such as "freebies" when he made that decision to not to get high anymore. But the more he said no, the less the temptations came.

You can't play around with fire. If you don't want to get burned, get away from the fire! You have to be like Joseph and flee the sin. You can't think of the "now" pleasure, but you must consider the end result. The more you say no to a drink or whatever the addiction might be, the further you will get away from it, and the more your will rise up and connect to your spirit man. As the soul and spirit get in agreement, so the body will obey.

You will get stronger each day as you step away. You are creating new strongholds with the Lord by replacing the old ones. You now must become just as obsessed with the Word of God as you were obsessed with the addiction.

Read 1 Corinthians 2:16. Some say Christianity is the great put on. Well then, put it on and act like it is so! As you take off filthy clothes and put on clean ones, do the same in the arena of your mind. Put on what is good and put off what is bad. Wash your mind with the Word of God. You can do it or God would not tell you to do it! He is a fair and just God. He shows you how to live in His Word.

Confession

I must allow a spiritual renewal to take place in my thoughts and attitudes. I must display this new nature because I am created in God's likeness. I am a new creature in Christ now. I have a new life. Therefore, I have new thoughts and actions. I have the mind of Christ. I present my body and my mind to Him because that is the least I can do for all He has done for me. He bought me with His blood.

I choose to think on the Word of God now. I will meditate on His Word day and night. It is my life now. I will hide His Words in my heart so I do not sin against Him. The Word of God is transforming my mind from the inside out. I have no desire for the old ways anymore. I think on higher ways now—His ways.

> Day #2: Proverbs 18:21 says, "Death and life are in the power of the tongue: and they that love it shall eat the fruit thereof." The most important part of our being is our mouths. What we say is vital because it comes out of our inner being, out of our mind's thoughts and emotions, which affects our will. Our will then determines how we are going to act and live out our lives. So our words do affect our lives!

If we realize that our words are the most powerful thing on this earth, we will be very careful what we speak. Words that are negative or tear down our self-esteem are words of death. If we believe words that people say to us such as, "You will never change and you will be an addict the rest of your life," if we embrace them, we will act like it is so. We will continue to live in that world we framed with our mouths or others framed for us. We have to reject negative thoughts and negative words. We cannot accept these kinds of thoughts and make them our own.

Don't allow other people to speak into your life. Let God speak into your mind instead. You are not an alcoholic, you are not an addict! You are not stuck in a distorted relationship with no way out. You are not stuck in compulsive eating or a spending disorder; you are not stuck! You are set free to live free and to worship the Almighty! You must put it in the past tense. If you keep speaking it in the present tense, you will not be free from those words and you will continue to believe you are not free.

Your words will actually hold you in bondage. Negative words create a prison cell—building those walls and bars up all around you. That is why it is so important to constantly be doing a "check up from the neck up"!

It is very important not to say, "Hi, I am Joe, an alcoholic." But instead say, "Hi, I am Joe, and I have been delivered from all addictions and I am a new creature in Christ Jesus! Old things have passed away and all things have become new in my life!"

We do not deny that Joe did have a problem, but if it isn't kept in the past it will still be a problem. You must believe you are a new person in Christ Jesus, that old things have passed and all things are new in your life. If you believe that, you will speak it and it will become a way of life for you. You will start to grow and gravitate towards the direction of your words! In Mark 9:23 Jesus says: _____

_____

_____

_____

_____

_____

_____

Write out 1 Corinthians 2:16 and make it personal by saying it to yourself at least five times.

_____

_____

Confession

I am the head and not the tail. I am above only and not beneath. I am on top of the mountain and not under it! I am victorious and not defeated. I am strong in the Lord and not relying on my own strength. I depend on His power that lives on the inside of me. I am strong and not weak. I am healed and not sick. I am prosperous and not poor. I have a sound mind and I am not losing it. I have a sharp memory and I use good judgment.

I have wisdom from God and I no longer make foolish decisions. I am loved and not rejected. I am full of God's joy and not sadness. My mind is at peace and I am not afraid. God's Word is alive, powerful, and working in me. I believe the Word of God and therefore, I speak it. His Word is working mightily in me and is continually setting me free! Jesus has set me free and so I am free indeed. Amen.

Day #3: Man is a tri-fold being. First Thessalonians 5:23 talks about man's being made up of three parts. What are the three parts of man? Write them out here: _____

_____

_____

God is also, a tri-fold being: Father, Son, and Holy Spirit. We are made in His image and likeness. We are made like Him. No other living creature is like God except man. Animals are only two part beings: soul and body. They do not have a spirit like we do.

When you realize how wonderfully made you are and that you can control your being, it is an awesome feeling. You are no longer powerless! The enemy wants you to think you're like an animal—controlled by the dictates of your flesh—but that is so far from the truth of who you are. You are made in the image of God, and He is no animal!

Genesis 1:26 and 2:7 says that you are made in the image of God and His likeness. He is your Father and you are His child. You are like Him.

Your mind is made up of three parts:

- Soul = thoughts and attitudes

- Emotions = feelings

- Your will = the determining factor or the decisions we make for our lives

Old habits may have been a source of pressure, pushing you from within to return to your old ways, but they are only the cravings of your body and the fleshly thoughts in your mind. These things can be controlled and subdued with God's power on the inside of you. If you have God's Word in your mind and your spirit man is already alive unto God, the majority will rule and your flesh will lose. Your mind and spirit will be in agreement, therefore your body must submit and obey what you tell it to do. The question is, "Are you controlling it?"

You release God's power by speaking His word out of your mouth. His Word has the power within it to change your life, to save your soul. It is a seed. It created you. You are a speaking spirit, like your Father God. Imitate Him. As He spoke, therefore you speak.

Read Genesis 1-2. How many times can you count "said," "speaking" or words that are related to talking in these chapters? We are to imitate our Father God and speak as He speaks.

Write out Ephesians 5:1 and explain what it means to you. _____

_____

_____

Confession

Greater is He that lives in me than he that is in the world. I will imitate my Father God and speak like He speaks. I frame my world with my words; therefore I call my world blessed. I am free from any domination of the enemy and nothing can control me anymore. I talk like Jesus talks. I speak life and not death.

Write out and say what you want in your life; frame your world with your words: _____

_____

_____

_____

_____

_____

_____

_____

_____

Day #4: Two great kings in the Bible were King Saul and King David. Saul was always fearful. He saw himself losing the kingdom and his throne, and so he did. He was appointed by God to be the first king over Israel. He loved God and knew of His ways, but he became puffed up in pride because he didn't judge himself and stay before God's presence. Soon other issues seeped in, such as fear, worry, anger, hatred, and even witchcraft. What is sad is that at any time, he could have called on God and repented to get his heart right but he, like so many others thought he could handle things just fine on his own. This is called pride. Pride says, "I don't need anyone's help; I can make it on my own." This is the worst sin of all!

We must come to the conclusion that without God, we cannot do anything! We must humble ourselves and call on His help for guidance in every situation of our lives. I think Saul's guard was also down, because in the beginning everything was going great. Then when troubles came, they came in like a flood. Saul was overwhelmed and caught off guard so he gave in to the pressure of all these things. He wasn't ready for the attacks of the enemy. In his leadership position, he should have been on his face several times a day before God. But instead, he was so confused that he ran to a witch for guidance. He had always relied on the prophet Samuel to pray for him and tell him what to do, but now that Samuel was gone—Saul was lost! Well, this was the last straw with God, and King Saul lost everything, including his life.

We cannot rely on others to carry us. We need to have a face to face relationship with God alone. We must take time to get to know our Heavenly Father. We must develop an intimate relationship with Him. We cannot rely on others to sustain us because they will eventually be gone, and then what will we do?

Psalm 27:4 says, "One thing have I desired of the Lord, that will I seek after; that I may dwell in the house of the Lord all the days of my life, to behold the beauty of the Lord, and to enquire in his temple." David longed to be in God's presence all the days of his life. He wanted to know God's ways. Praising the Lord sustained him during difficult times of loneliness.

The second king, David, was a young man after God's own heart. He loved to be in God's presence and to sing to Him daily. He was too young to go to war with his older brothers so he tended to his dad's sheep and wrote songs. He had a lot of quiet time to talk to God, and he actually liked it that way. When he had to visit his brothers at the war camp to take them food, he was amazed at how the big giant Goliath was cussing everyone out and scaring the entire army of Israel. He was so mad that he decided to go after the enemy himself!

He had experienced God's help when he fought off a lion and a bear. With boldness, he believed he could do anything, so he went after the giant Goliath! In the natural, it looked like a joke—a seventeen year old boy running after a giant, screaming God's Word and twirling a slingshot. But we all know the outcome. With God's Word in our mouths and backing us, we can face any giant in our lives just like David did! Nothing is too hard for our God!

David's faith confession in 1 Samuel 17:45-46 says: _____

_____

_____

_____

_____

_____

First Samuel 17:47 says, "And all this assembly shall know that the Lord saveth not with sword and spear: for the battle is the Lord's, and he will give you into our hands." God doesn't deal with our enemies like we do. God says we are not to strive with people;

we are not to fight with flesh and blood. We are to look beyond the natural and speak His Word into the unseen spirit world and watch the angels go to work on our behalf. We fight the good fight of faith, and then we watch God watch over His Word to bring it to pass. We attack the enemy with our weapon—speaking the Word of God. We say, no to addictions once and for all and they have to go, in Jesus' name!"

It is true that we can do nothing without God. Our Father God takes on our battles when we serve Him. We are His children and no one messes with God's kids! So start believing that God loves you and wants to deliver you from everything that is harmful and unclean. You can live a life drug-free! You can live a life co-dependent no more, and yes, you can start today!

If you can see it, then you can have it!

Write out Ephesians 6:12:_____

_____

_____

_____

_____

_____

_____

Day #5: Read Numbers 13:1-33 about those who had a different spirit. Moses sent spies to check out the Promised Land. Out of the twelve, only two came back with a good report: Joshua and Caleb. Write down what they said that made them different. _____

_____

_____

_____

_____

The other ten said, "The enemy is strong and powerful." They were already seeing, believing, and sealing their fate with their words. In verse 28, the spies said these things:

- they are a strong and powerful people

- their city has giant walls

- we saw the sons of Anak (the giants) dwelling with them

They were coming up with all the reasons why it looked impossible take the land that God promised. They were moved by the natural circumstances of what they saw and how they felt. And guess what? That is what they spoke! Their words immobilized them with fear so they were powerless to go in and possess their promises form God.

Psalm 27:13 says, "I had fainted, unless I had believed to see the goodness of the Lord in the land of the living." We don't faint or quit or give up, never! The Israelites were giving up and that would mean they would not receive their inheritance and the blessings that God had for them. They allowed fear to come into their hearts and minds, and then reinforced it with their words. They believed in their hearts, therefore they spoke it! They reasoned it all away with natural logical thinking. But God's way doesn't always make sense. It is supernatural and we can live a life of the miraculous if we dare to believe it!

When it looks impossible, that's when God will tell you it is possible!

Without a word from God, you have nothing to step out on. Faith acts on what it hears. You believe something in your heart and then you act on it. Romans 10:9-10 says, "That if thou shalt confess with thy mouth the Lord Jesus, and shalt believe in thine heart that

God hath raised him from the dead, thou shalt be saved. For with the heart man believeth unto righteousness; and with the mouth confession is made unto salvation." This is how we got saved, and it is how we continue to walk the Christian walk.

Find your scripture to stand on. Nothing has changed from day one. Dare to believe God at His Word, then confess it and act like it is so!

Hebrews 11:6 says, "But without faith it is impossible to please him." Faith is just believing God's Word and doing it. We live this way, day by day. It is our life now.

Confession

I believe in my heart and confess with my mouth that Jesus Christ is my Lord and Savior. I also believe and confess with my mouth that Father God heals me, delivers me, helps me, prospers me, strengthens me, and protects me. He is El Shaddai, the God who is more than enough. I am ever thankful. If God says that I am well able to overtake the giants in the land, then I am going to do just that! I am well able to overtake any enemy or giant that stands in my way. Amen.

Day #6: Read and write out 2 Corinthians 10:3-5.

_____

_____

_____

_____

_____

_____

_____

_____

_____

_____

_____

_____

_____

_____

_____

_____

_____

I cast down imaginations and things that would not bring glory
to God in my thought life. I choose, as an act of my free will, to think
on things that are pure, holy, lovely, and of a good report and in line
with His will. His Word is His Will. I will not allow strongholds of
unforgiveness, fear, doubt or worry to build up in my mind. Instead,
I rebuke them and cast them down at the feet of Jesus. I then replace
them with scriptures that promise me otherwise. I know my Father
God wants good for me, and it starts with me choosing to believe that.
I choose to receive it. I choose life. (Read Deuteronomy 28:1-15 and
30:14-20)

Psalm 103:1-5 tells about all the benefits that God has for us.
Write them out:

_____

_____

_____

_____

_____

_____

_____

_____

_____

_____

_____

_____

_____

_____

_____

_____

_____

_____

Day #7: The Word of God anchors my soul, producing in me a sound mind. Ephesians 4:14 says God doesn't want me to be what? _____

_____

_____

_____ Why? Because He wants us to become stable, not up and down. When we are unstable, our thoughts are always changing; they are not established so we become unpredictable. No one ever knows what we are going to say or do next. This was the behavior of our old man, but now we are new creations

in Christ Jesus. Say: I have put off the old man and put
on the new man in Christ Jesus. I am established and
rooted in Christ. I am not up and down anymore because
I am stable now.

We need to grow up spiritually in Christ. We need to grow up and
submit to the Word of God. Once we do this, His Word will anchor our
thoughts and emotions and will help us stand strong. (Read James.)
Write out James 1:8.

_____

_____

_____

_____

Don't be of a double mind or you will not receive anything from
the Lord. We cannot be saying one thing and doing another. It
doesn't work that way. Have you ever heard the saying, "I can't hear
what you are saying because your actions are speaking too loudly?"
Watch how a person acts and that is how really are. We believe and
therefore we speak and most of all, do. What we fill our minds with is
what we will say and do!

If we pray for something and don't find a scripture to back it up,
then when the pressures of life and the devil come, we will lose it. We
need to bind our prayers and desires to the Word of God and stand
on His Word. It has to become a way of life to us, not just some magic
words like "abracadabra." God is not a quick fix. He wants your whole
life, after all He gave you His! Recovery takes time. It took time to get
into an addiction, so it will also take time to get out.

One of my spiritual mentors in the faith, Kenneth E. Hagin,
always said, "I can locate people's faith immediately by their words.

If they're in fear, then it will come out of their mouth." Doubt, unforgiveness, worry, pride, or lust—will all be revealed! A person will start talking what they have meditated on! And guess what? Their actions will follow!

What are you speaking? Do you know you first thought it? That is why it is so important to speak God's Word. You will start believing it, and then you will begin doing it. This is how our minds are transformed—one day at a time, one milestone at a time!

Don't tell yourself anymore that you are an addict or have a drinking problem. When you do this, you keep telling yourself you're not free so you can't get free. Stop, think, and then speak. What is it that you want? Speak the desired result. Speak the answer. Eventually your heart will begin to believe it. Your life will start to head in the direction that you begin to focus on as it manifests in the natural realm. Start in the spirit and watch it produce in the natural. Prove God at His Word!

Read Luke 11:17-26 about what happens if you don't fill yourself up with the Word of God. Then read Luke 4:1-15 about how Jesus was tempted and how he handled the devil. What were three ways that He was tempted? _____

_____

_____

_____

_____

What did He tell the devil every time that caused him to flee and leave Jesus alone?_____

_____

What must you do to get the devil to leave you alone? _____

_____

Take a few minutes to write out and then speak the Word of God to the devil, telling him to leave your life and your family's lives. _____

_____

_____

_____

_____

_____

In Luke 11, when the man did not fill his house up with the Word of God, what happened to him? _____

_____

This can happen to anyone of us if we don't take recovery seriously. The enemy is out to destroy us any way he can. So be on guard and put on your armor (Ephesians 6:12- 18), then the wicked one cannot touch you! (Read Mark 4 - Parable of the Sower)

Confession

I am the righteousness of God in Christ Jesus. The Greater One lives in me. I have been bought with the blood of Jesus Christ. He is my Lord. I am redeemed from the power of the wicked one, Satan. He has no control over me. I am redeemed from the curse of the law. I am redeemed from sin, sickness and disease. I resist the devil and he must flee from me. I am full of God's Word. When the enemy tries to harass me, all he will hear is the word of God from my lips. My mind is renewed by the Word of God. Every time I speak it, I become stronger than before. I am a winner! I am victorious through Christ. I am not a loser. I am good ground for the Word of God to grow in me.

I meditate on God's Word all day long. I speak it in every area of my life, and my life is conforming to it. I am getting stronger day by day. I know who I am now. I am a child of God. I have the power to change my life. God has given it to me. I change it first by choosing Jesus as my Lord and Savior. Then I submit to the Word of God and speak it into my life. I am free from addictions because I choose to be free. I want to be free! Therefore, I choose life and not death. I will live and not die and declare the works of the Lord forever! Amen.

NOTES

_____

_____

_____

_____

_____

_____

_____

_____

_____

_____

_____

_____

_____

_____

_____

_____

_____

_____

MILESTONE #11 FRIEND OR FOE?

The eleventh milestone is that I need divine intervention concerning the company I keep. It is vital that I surround myself with safe godly people who can assist me in my recovery. Old associates will only trip me up, so I must stay far from them.

Even if you have been clean for a while, if you are not particular about whom you allow to get close to you, it could be just a matter of time before you end up back in old behavioral patterns—saying and doing things you vowed never to do again. It will be very difficult, if not impossible, to stay sober and straight when you become too comfortable with sinners. (Read Psalm 1).

We are "birds of a feather." That means that like spirits hang out together. There is an old proverb that says, "If you want to know what a man is like then look at the company he keeps." As a school teacher, I can remember discussions in the teacher's lounge about students who started to go downhill in their grades, personal hygiene, and attitude. We always knew it had a direct correlation to the people they were now calling friends.

A person will surround himself with the people he feels comfortable with and who are like him, but this will not be a good thing if their minds have not been renewed to the Word of God. That's why you see Christians and wonder to yourself, Why are they with people like that? Can't they see that they are unsafe? No, they can't see or they don't want to see! If they are not filtering everything through the Word of God, then they definitely can't see. They will live out of the flesh or the dictates of their cravings and desires. They will make bad choices and be stuck once again in nightmare relationships. The enemy never ceases to try to trip us up in this area. Never!

In recovery, it is vital that we change the people we call our friends. We are new creatures in Christ Jesus. We have new habits and a new lifestyle, and most of all, we must have new friends. People who were once our close "party buddies" will have to be kept at a distance in order for us to maintain sobriety and holiness. This could even include family members. If you do not heed this warning, it will be like throwing yourself back into the frying pan and it will be just a matter of time before you burn! The Bible says to flee youthful lusts and people who will not influence you to do what is right, good, pure, holy, and acceptable in His sight. A sign of true recovery is when you are able to stay away from such people and don't even have the desire to be around them.

> Day #1: Today is the beginning of the rest of my life. I will not leave here like I came, in Jesus' name. I have made a decision to change, and God is helping me. I am not alone. God's people are helping me. And most of all, I am helping myself. Because I have been set free and I intend to stay free! Amen.

Second Corinthians 6:14-18 says, "Be ye not unequally yoked together with unbelievers: for what fellowship hath righteousness with unrighteousness? and what communion hath light with darkness? And what concord hath Christ with Belial? or what part hath he that believeth with an infidel? And what agreement hath the temple of God with idols? for ye are the temple of the living God; as God hath said, I will dwell in them, and walk in them; and I will be their God, and they shall be my people. Wherefore come out from among them, and be ye separate, saith the Lord, and touch not the unclean thing; and I will receive you. And will be a Father unto you, and ye shall be my sons and daughters, saith the Lord Almighty."

Read 2 Corinthians 6 and 1 Corinthians 6. These chapters are about relationships and not being defiled. Who are our friends and who are our foes? James 4:4 says that if you are friends with the world, then you are an enemy of God. First John 3:16-18 says that those who do not obey God's laws, love other Christians, and don't give to them in their time of need are not children of God. Therefore, they are enemies of God. When you love someone, you want to be around them and you do what they like to do. You want to give to them. God's love is the same, always giving.

In Matthew 7:21, Jesus tells us what to look for in choosing friends. See what kind of fruit they are producing in their lives, for many say they are Christians, but it is their lifestyle that will prove it.

There are those who appear religious, but God says He doesn't know them. Learn the difference between spiritual and religious. These people look like they love God. They raise their hands in church. They know all the songs, quote scriptures, and seem to talk the right talk. But their walk is far from Him! They cheat, lie, cuss, and swindle. They yield to the nature of their flesh—drinking and having sexual misconduct, yet they still expect to be blessed of the Lord. Then they say they are covered under grace. There is grace and mercy for the one who repents and truly wants to change. But grace is not a license to sin. It is the power of God to enable us to rise above that sin and be able to resist it!

If anyone is not living for God, professing Him as Lord in word or deed, he is serving the devil. Satan is our foe! In the book of James, God says that He resists the proud but gives grace to the humble. Whoever loves this world more than God is the enemy of God and therefore our enemy. I know this is heavy, but it is the Word of God! If you don't take this seriously, the devil will trip you up in this area. You must be like Joseph and flee sin, even the appearances of it—at all costs!

How do we handle peer pressure? We handle it by not forgetting our purpose. Genesis 37:5 says Joseph had a _____ . But Joseph also had to _____. (On your own time, slowly read and ponder the life of Joseph in Genesis 37-49.) Joseph's life was full of unfairness, pressures, temptations, and tragedies—one after another. If it wasn't for God speaking to him in a dream and planting a purpose in him to keep his heart focused, I don't know if he would have made it. You must have a dream to pursue or life becomes meaningless. Our purpose is the "why" of our existence.

When God gives us a dream, we must go after it no matter what the cost! The cost, a lot of times, will mean cutting off relationships that interfere and are unhealthy to our spiritual well-being. There will always be people, places and things sent by the enemy to cause us to get off course. Just as God sends people to help us, our foe Satan sends people our way to mess us up.

Joseph endured these three things:

- _____

- _____

- _____

But when it was all over with, Joseph was living in the

_____ . And you can, too! Your life can change and
be so transformed that you are living a life that you only dreamed you
could live. God wants this for you. He wants His very best for you.
The question is, "how much do you want it for you? Enough to say
good bye to people with no future and no focus? I hope so! Learn to
say no! No is a healthy boundary word. It is the first boundary word
we learn as kids. And it gets easier as you practice it. Yes, it is okay
as a Christian to say no! In fact, you will need to use this word often!
Saying "no" to unhealthy situations, saying "no" to unsafe people,
saying no to temptation, and saying no to sin, is a must to if you
are to stay pure before God. You may even have to even say 'no' to
friends, if they are distracting you from spending time with God and
you're not taking care of your regular responsibilities. Do the right
thing! God is with you and He will help you. It will get easier the
more you say 'no' and do what is right! Besides, healthy friends will
understand and respect your boundaries.

We must finish our race. Read Genesis 41:38-41. Joseph finished
his purpose. He was put in charge of all of Egypt to save the rest of
the world, especially his own family. Family is not supposed to be the
enemy, but a lot of times they can be used by Satan to interfere with
God's plan. Joseph told the wrong people his dream. Even though
they were family, they weren't for him, but against him.

We must be careful whom we confide in as well. Not everyone is
for our recovery and wholeness. Remember, you don't need to tell
all your secrets. Some matters are just between you and God.

Joseph did obey God and eventually, all was restored. His broken
relationship with his brothers was restored. Joseph was an example
of someone who painfully endured to the end. He never gave up, he

never gave in, and he never quit believing in his purpose. We have to be like this when it comes to holiness and doing right—no matter what the cost!

Examples

Samson is an example of someone who didn't finish his course. Some say it was because of his permissive parents. They never taught him healthy boundaries. They spoiled him by giving him whatever he demanded, instead of putting him in his place to preserve his calling. He had no self-control or restraints with women, and he couldn't get a grip on his lust problem on his own.

He didn't guard his eyes. He looked at what he liked to look at, therefore, he fed his flesh. He lived for himself and it cost him his vision. He didn't just lose his natural eyesight, but he also lost the vision of who he was in God. At the end of his life, he was only able to regain some of that vision. His life was cut short. It cost him everything—the anointing on his life, his reputation, and the relationships God meant for him.

People lost respect for the man of God. He is more remembered for his lust for ungodly women than his supernatural strength. His testimony was marred, but was given as a lesson for us to learn what not to do. His life shows us what happens to those who give into their flesh and live for instant gratification. They can't say 'no' to unhealthy people and lifestyles. Samson lost everything by confiding in the wrong people. It cost him dearly! He chose to trust others instead of trusting in God.

Moses was a godly example of someone who refused to have it all when he realized it would compromise his calling. He didn't go the way of the world. He even turned down palace living! But his name still became greater than all the pharaohs of his time. We still know about his deeds today. When he found out his true heritage or purpose, nothing could corrupt it.

Moses forsook all to know God. The Bible says he lacked nothing! God always provided supernaturally. His life affected a nation (his true family) and his obedience to God led them out of captivity. They saw what he sacrificed and dared to believe in a better life, too. He gave his life for others and God restored everything back to him. He lived a long satisfying life. But it doesn't say that about those who stayed in Egypt and lived to satisfy their lusts; they died!

Moses is an example of one who, like Joseph, suffered great trials but still finished his purpose. He was raised by a heathen princess, but he didn't use that as an excuse why he couldn't succeed in life. His circumstances didn't keep him down.

So what caused Joseph and Moses to keep going? They prospered because they kept fixed on their purpose, the race that was set before them. They were careful who they spent their time with, surrounding themselves with God's people who would help them accomplish their purpose. Samson didn't stay focused on his calling; he was out for pleasure. He did not respect the anointing that was on his life so he lost it all. His life was tragically cut short, even though he killed more people in his death than in his whole lifetime.

Confession

I have the wisdom and discernment of God living on the inside of me. I make wise choices and shun bad ones. I choose godly companions so I can learn and grow through these healthy relationships. I flee youthful lusts, in Jesus' name. I walk in the

Spirit and not in the flesh. I ask You Lord, and I thank You for placing a hedge of thorns around me that keeps seducing spirits far from me. I am no longer deceived! The rest of my life is set apart to live in holiness as I live to fulfill Your purpose for my life from this day forward, in Jesus' name. Amen.

Day #2: Proverbs 18:24 says, "A man that hath friends must shew himself friendly: and there is a friend that sticketh closer than a brother." That person who is closer than a brother is Jesus. So if we don't have friends or it takes time to make some new friends, we still have Jesus. He is always near and waiting for us to tell Him our intimate secrets. And He will be around long after our friends come and go! It is said that we have only five close friends in our lifetime, but Jesus is a friend who is there for all of eternity. People come and go and we do not know how long they will be in our lives. It may just be for a season. So cherish God's people as they are passing through and then let them go! It is good to show ourselves friendly, but not to the wrong people.

We can't just hook up with anyone like we used to do. I used to think that I had no choice and had to befriend everyone I met because it must be right because they are in my realm of influence such as my neighbors, job and classmates. I hate to say this, but I now know the enemy can send people across our pathway as well. We can gravitate back to old familiar spirits and not realize it if we are not walking in the Spirit of God. We can be with the same kind of people, just in different bodies and in a different location.

For a while until we grow strong in the Lord, we may not be able to trust our own judgment. Look where it got us in the past! Pray and ask God to send some godly friends your way. People who love God and will care about you are friends you need in your life now. The Christian walk can be a lonely walk at times, because not everyone will be excited about your desire to live for Christ. They'll even accuse you of trying to act better than them. You may even be called "holier than thou," among other things.

People who don't celebrate your recovery must be kept at a distance. There are those whom we call acquaintances and there are those whom we call friends. Acquaintances must be kept at a distance, but you don't have to be rude to them. Be cordial and polite. Say hello and bye, but don't hang out with them! Don't call people who are living ungodly your friends. Don't call your old drinking and party buddies your friends. You do not have the same things in common anymore. What do Christ and Satan have in common or light and darkness have in common? This is vital in recovery if you want to stay clean.

Friends of the past are just that—in your past. You must move forward now. Ask yourself these questions if you are not sure: "Are they friend or foe? Do they live for God or the devil? Are they walking in the light of God's Word or are they still living in the darkness of sin and death?" If you still don't know, ask a person of God to help you. A lot times we can't see as clearly as others can see from the outside looking in. This could also include family members. You can't even attend a family function if you know it will jeopardize your sobriety because there is going to be a bunch of drinking there. You will have to act like Joseph did and flee.

Beware of the triggers: situations, people, places, and things that cause you to respond in a manner that pulls you back into the old lifestyle. You cannot afford this, for if you slip, it could take years to recover—if you ever do recover! I have seen this happen too often!

Write out the things that have been triggers in your life: ____

_____

_____

_____

_____

_____

_____

Write out Proverbs 13:20.

_____

_____

_____

_____

Those who drink until they vomit or pass out are not wise. Those who blow their paychecks in one night to spend time out with "buddies" are not wise. A wise man says "I am going home tonight after work." A wise man will take a sack lunch and eat at his desk if it means he will miss going out to lunch that involves afternoon cocktails with the staff. Are you a wise person or a foolish one? What are some situations you know you must avoid in your everyday life?

Confession

I show myself friendly, therefore I have friends. I give and it is given unto me. I allow the love of God to shine through me. I walk in the Spirit and not in the flesh. I have wisdom to know who should be my close companions and who should just be an acquaintance. I am not deceived and I am not desperate just to hook up with anyone.

Jesus is my best friend. When I feel lonely, I can spend time with Him. He is my Shepherd, therefore I have no lack. I am wise and not foolish. When I was a child, I spoke and acted like a child, but now I have put away foolish ways. I am strong in the Lord and know who I am in Christ. Greater is He who lives in me than he who lives in this world. I am a friend of God. Amen.

Day #3: Separate and sanctify yourselves. Read 1 Corinthians 6:9-20. Write out what it means to you:

_____

_____

_____

_____

_____

_____

_____

_____

_____

_____

_____

Verse 17 says we are _____ own any more.

Verse 19 says our body is _____. Verse 18 says to do what? _____. You have been blood bought; you are not your own to do as you please anymore. Your job is to keep yourself holy now. Write out what 2 Corinthians 6:14-18 means to you. _____

_____

_____

_____

_____

_____

What do light and darkness have in common? _____

_____

What does "unequally yoked to unbelievers" mean to you? ___

_____

_____

_____

Verse 16 says you are the _____

_____. So you cannot defile yourself with idols. What does

that mean to you? _____

In verses 16-18, God said He will do this if you do what?

_____

Read 1 Corinthians 9:22-27. Paul says he does this so that
he won't be considered a castaway or one that is disqualified
from the race—that people can't receive from him. Write what
he means by this.

_____

_____

_____

_____

_____

_____

_____

_____

_____

_____

_____

_____

We must have this attitude that Paul displayed to be able to press forward and finish our race in life. What kind of attitude did Paul have? _____

_____

_____

Confession

I refuse to defile myself with the world. I am a child of righteousness. I am holy, set apart for the work of the Lord now. I walk in the light as He is in the light. I shun the works of darkness. I no longer have anything in common with those who walk in darkness and live in sin. The Lord has set me free from darkness and I am free indeed. I now walk in the light, as He is in the light. I choose to present my body to the Lord as a living sacrifice, for that is my reasonable service to please Him. I don't live to please the flesh and sin, I live to be holy and walk in the Spirit. Amen.

> Day #4: When we were users and abusers, our relationships were out of whack! We didn't know how to prioritize who was important and how to establish safe boundaries for our lives. We did not know how to pick healthy, safe people to befriend. So now we must learn

how to prioritize our life and choose good relationships.

Setting Healthy Priorities in Relationships

1. God is first! Spend time with Him every day through prayer and reading His Word.

2. Take time alone for yourself so you have something to give to others.

3. Your spouse is next. Spend time together, even if it is only 10 minutes, just holding hands or sitting together watching television. Make sure you say nice things to each other.

4. Children in the home are your principle concern. Try to do something with them each day that is fun, besides correction. Start their day off with good words of how proud you are of them or things like this. Tell them how you love them because these words will linger all day. Help them with their homework and chores. Let them know you care about them. (If your children don't live with you, call them as much as possible to keep the relationship active.)

5. Parents, grandparents and other kin are important. Do weekly to quarterly contacts by phone calls or notes to stay in touch as much as possible. Don't forget birthdays!

6. Neighbors, coworkers or people at school are around you all day—and you have no choice, they are just there! Use wisdom in what you say and do. Do your work as unto the Lord, on the job and even around the house. Remember, people are always watching you.

7. Friends and people at church are the healthy people in your life. Treasure and value each friendship as a gift from the

Lord. Stay in touch weekly and do things together at least twice a month to develop and maintain the friendship. Be around those who celebrate you and enjoy your company. Don't be around those who tolerate you or you are trying to force the relationship and they are not. Not everyone will want to be your friend. Get over it and move on to those who do! Your friends should mainly come from where you worship, fellowship, or volunteer in your home church.

Write out Hebrews 10:25.

_____

_____

_____

_____

_____

_____

Your friends should be fellow Christians. You have to change who you surround yourself with in order for your life to change. This is vital! Get involved in church activities. Meet new friends by showing yourself friendly. Notice where friends rank in this list of priorities? They are not before the Lord or before your spouse and family anymore! In fact, if you are married, your best friend should be your spouse. (Read Ephesians 5 and 6 about family relationships)

Confession

Lord, I thank You for helping me to prioritize relationships. I ask You to give me a desire to put my loved ones in the proper perspective. They deserve it. I am not an island unto myself. I need them and I need Your people in my life. And in Jesus' name, they all need me! I ask that You give me wisdom so I will have discernment to know who I can allow to get close to me and who I cannot afford to let get near. I now desire to make good choices in my companions. I receive the godly friends You have ready to hook up with me, in Jesus' name, because I know they are vital in my recovery process. I need them; I cannot make it alone. I have You inside me, I have Your Holy Spirit empowering me, and I have Your people encouraging me. I can do all things, in Jesus' name. Hallelujah!

Day #5: These are scriptures about friends. Write them out and meditate on them.

Proverbs 17:17:

_____

_____

_____

_____

Proverbs 27:6:

_____

_____

_____

_____

Proverbs 27:9:

_____

_____

_____

_____

John 15:13-14:

_____

_____

_____

_____

1 Peter 1:22:

_____

_____

_____

_____

Hebrews 13:1:

_____

_____

_____

_____

Galatians 6:2:

_____

_____

_____

_____

Ecclesiastes 4: 9-10:

_____

_____

_____

_____

1 Corinthians 1:10:

_____

_____

_____

_____

1 Corinthians 15:33:

_____

_____

_____

_____

Amos 3:3: _____

_____

_____

_____

James 4:4:

_____

_____

_____

_____

1 Corinthians 15:33:

_____

_____

_____

_____

Describe your ideal friend:

_____

_____

_____

_____

Confession

Jesus, You are my Lord. I trust in You with all my heart. You are my Savior and my closest friend. You are there for me when it seems like no one else cares. Thank You for believing in me and not giving up on me. Thank You for helping me to become more like You. I ask You to help me to become a loyal and faithful friend to the ones You do bring into my life. I want to be trustworthy to someone. I can be a good friend with Your help and strength in me. I will not burn bridges anymore if the people are good and godly, because I need them in my life. I will allow others to get close, and I thank You in advance for helping me to trust again. Amen.

Day #6: It is so important to be in the right company—God's company. When things go wrong, the family of

God is your true family. When a real crisis occurs, they will know how to stand with you in faith and encourage you in the Lord. And most of all, they will pray with you. When one or more get together in prayer with you, things happen!

Acts 3 tells about Peter and John (two brethren in Christ hanging out together). They were just going to the temple for prayer when a lame beggar sitting at the gate asked them for money. Peter responded with this famous quote in verse 6, "Silver and gold have I none; but such as I have give I thee: In the name of Jesus Christ of Nazareth rise up and walk."

The man got healed and it created such a stir among the people that it also opened the door for Peter to preach to a lot of others about Jesus! This upset the religious leaders so much that they had Peter and John arrested for disrupting their services. Acts 4:23 tells us when they were released from jail, they returned back to their own company. If you continue to read on, in Acts 4 it tells us how their family in the Lord embraced them, prayed with them, and strengthened them in the Lord.

Acts 4:31-32 says, "And when they had prayed, the place was shaken where they were assembled together; and they were all filled with the Holy Ghost, and they spake the word of God with boldness. And the multitude of them that believed were of one heart and of one soul: neither said any of them that ought of the things which he possessed was his own; but they had all things common."

Apparently, there were new followers joining their company after the miracles happened and the people heard for the first time, someone "real" preaching with authority. Many people got filled with the Holy Spirit. There was unity among the brethren. When Peter and John were arrested, they didn't get mad at God, but instead they rejoiced knowing more would come to know God because of it!

It is important that we don't retreat when things look bleak or seem to go wrong, especially if we know we are doing the right thing and things still go wrong. We must not pull away from the family of God and forsake attending church. Do not forsake being in the house of God, but go and become of one heart and soul with your Christian family. Sing and worship God, get filled with the Holy Spirit if you have not already been baptized with the Holy Spirit, or just get recharged in the Spirit so you can be strengthened for the days ahead. God will help you—but you must get in position!

Write out why the company you keep is so important in your walk with God. _____

_____

_____

_____

_____

_____

_____

_____

Confession

Lord, I thank You that You are for me, that You are with me, and that You live in me. I am not alone. You send Your people to comfort me and most of all, I have the Holy Spirit living on the inside of me, who is the greatest comforter of all. When things happen beyond my control, I will seek out help from my brethren in Christ. I will go to my own company and not try to handle things on my own.

I need to be among my family, the body of Christ. I need the corporate anointing that comes from us all praying and joining together as one heart and one soul. I long to be in Your house Father, singing praises to Your name. Hallelujah! Psalm 27:4 says "One thing have I desired of the Lord, that will I seek after; that I may dwell in the house of the Lord all the days of my life, to behold the beauty of the Lord, and to enquire in his temple.

> Day #7: The book of Proverbs is about two men: one who is foolish and one who is wise. It even sheds light on two other kinds of men. The scorner is the one who is beyond foolishness and is hardened in his heart. The simpleton is the one who has the potential to become wise, but needs lots of help because he lacks knowledge.

These types of people represent how people live. They also display levels of a person's walk and integrity with God. Here are the following types in more depth:

1. The Simpleton – does foolish things because he lacks knowledge and is easily swayed. One could say that he is gullible. He lacks discernment and can be easily taken advantage of, especially by the scorner. There is a lot of hope for this person once he is anchored in the Word of God. Children would fall into this category, as well as new believers.

2. Foolish Man – is one who falls down repeatedly because he hasn't learned certain lessons. He has moved beyond simplicity and innocence to deliberate wrongdoing. He tastes

rebellion and likes it! He seems to have very little spiritual sensitivity and is always justifying his way of doing things. He challenges authority and is not shrewd like the scorner; he freely flaunts everything he thinks and does. Again, knowledge is the key, but along with it, this person will need life experiences or consequences. Most likely he didn't have many of these as a child. Hopefully after enough of the consequences, he will humble himself and become like the simpleton, a child, and start believing and trusting. If not, he could eventually progress to the scorner category—which is not good at all!

3. The Scorner —despises counsel, although he will act like he loves it. He is a deceiver. He sows strife among the brethren. He actually hates those who love him. He is shrewd and manipulates the simpleton and the foolish to accomplish his goals. He worms his way into gullible Christian's lives and takes from them. Although, because of his cunning craftiness (has had much practice), others don't even realize it at first or even link him to any wrongdoing. He loves to go to church, but not for the purpose of submitting or worship. He wants to be seen and heard as someone important, and usually will be in some leadership capacity if spiritual discernment has not been exercised. He is in the category of the wolf in sheep's clothing. Beware! His heart is not for you or with you. His heart is not for God or the things of God. His heart is only for himself.

4. The Wise Man – the one who has learned life's lessons and is progressing forward to become all God wants him to be. He has left the simple and foolish ways behind. Since he protects his heart from bitterness and unforgiveness, he escapes the

route of the scorner. The wise man is still growing daily. He hears the Word, believes it and then does it. He acts like the Word is so! He becomes even wiser as time passes on. He is able to handle more responsibility because he has proven himself faithful. He heeds warnings, avoids temptations, chooses wise companions, surrounds himself with those of like faith, loves God and His Holy Word, cares about the brethren and displays attributes of God's love in his personal life. He is a person of integrity and high moral ethics. He can see right through the scorner most of the time, therefore the scorner avoids getting close to him so he won't be exposed. He doesn't even want to make eye contact! Jesus refers to the wise man over and over again as the man who hears and does God's Word. (Some of these analogies were paraphrased and ideas came from the book: Sowing for Excellence (Educating God's Way) by Claude Schindler.)

Which man are you? Hopefully, your goal is to be on the pathway of the wise man. Psalm 1 mentions all these types of people. Read it and write what it means to you:

_____

_____

_____

_____

The Bible tells us in Proverbs 1 that the way we get wisdom is how? _____

_____

What does James 1 say about wisdom? _____

_____

_____

_____

_____

Confession

Lord, I ask that You open the eyes of my understanding so I will not be deceived. Help me to always judge myself so my heart never becomes hardened. Show me when I am wrong so that I can change the error of my ways. I ask for wisdom above all else, for then I will hear Your voice and know Your ways.

When I start to go down the wrong path, Holy Spirit, I ask You to intervene and help me so I don't make wrong choices. I hear my Father's voice and the voice of the stranger I will not follow. I am not led astray. I know the will of my Father and I walk it out all the days of my life, in Jesus' name. He guides me and leads me by His right hand of righteousness. I am in His hands and I am not relying on my own understanding or wisdom. I hear and I obey, in Jesus' name. Amen.

NOTES

_____

_____

_____

_____

_____

_____

_____

_____

_____

_____

_____

_____

_____

_____

_____

_____

_____

_____

_____

MILESTONE #12 BEING A GIVER AND NOT A TAKER

The twelfth milestone is that I need divine intervention to learn how to be a giver, instead of always thinking someone owes me something. The world is always saying, "My name is Jimmy, and I will take all you gimme!" But we should be saying as Christians, "How can I give? What can I do to make a difference in the life of another?" This is the love of God, caring for others. God is a giver and not a taker! "There are those who are moochers," says Pastor Willie George who pastors the largest church in Tulsa, "and moochers are never givers! Just as givers are never moochers!"

For so long, our dysfunctional lifestyle was one of mooching, manipulating, conning, swindling, or doing whatever it took to survive—especially if it was to get that next high. We never even considered another human being's needs. It was all about me, myself, and I. There wasn't room for anyone else in our world. We would even rob our own children or mother if we got that desperate!

But now that we are in Christ Jesus, we have put off that former lifestyle. We have put to death that old man. My new man has been made alive in Christ Jesus! We don't live like we used to live, to take from others. It is not even in our nature to do so anymore because we have been set free.

We are no longer users of mankind, instead we live to give. We are not out to see what we can get, but we live out the rest of our lives to be a blessing, contributing to society by working with our hands and giving from our hearts with pure motives. As Father God has given to us, so we in turn can give to others. We show mercy as mercy has been shown to us. We are learning a great truth—it truly is better to give than to receive but the secret is, you have to have it to give it! God wouldn't make you give what you didn't have!

We are excited about this new life in Christ. By taking our minds off of ourselves, we can see the world around us a lot clearer. We do have something to contribute; we have something this world needs. People are waiting on us!

God has positioned all of us in certain walks of life (our realm of influence) and it is there that we can make a difference. (Unless He calls you out of it.) That is your place called "there" and He is obliged to take care of you when you're in your place!

> Day #1: Today is the beginning of the rest of my life. I will not leave here like I came, in Jesus name. I have made a decision to change and God is helping me! I am not alone. God's people are helping me. And most of all, I am helping myself! Because I have been set free, I intend to stay free! Amen.

Galatians 6:7-11 says, "Be not deceived; God is not mocked: for whatsoever a man soweth, that shall he also reap. For he that soweth to his flesh shall of the flesh reap corruption; but he that soweth to the Spirit shall of the Spirit reap life everlasting. And let us not be weary in well doing; for in due season we shall reap, if we faint not. As we have therefore opportunity, let us do good unto all men, especially unto them who are of the household of faith."

In verse 7 it says, you can be deceived but don't be anymore. And don't you be the deceiver, like I know some of us have done in the past. Be honest now, even if it hurts! There should be no more lying to cover up the other lies. Be around those who are honest, pattern yourself after them. Be around honest people and you will want to be honest. Be around dishonest people and you will be like them. We are known by the company that we keep!

- Work with your hands - get a job! Stop expecting to be taken care of. You take care of you. Stop trying to mooch off of the system or off of other Christians.

- Don't hurt people with your mouth. You do not have to live on the defensive any more. No more living in the "payback" mode.

- Don't manipulate to get your way. Don't take and take. Live to give.

Sure, sometimes you may need help, but that shouldn't be the norm in your life anymore. Everything shouldn't be a crisis where someone has to come to your rescue or bail you out of your messes all the time. Instead, you should be helping others.

It is true that we do reap what we sow, and we have probably heard that a lot in the negative connotation. Let's sow good seeds now, so that goodness will come back to us. And of course, treat your brethren as your new family whom you love and care about!

You are no longer living in survival mode. God is and will take care of you now. He knows what you need Matthew 6:32.

- Let people see that you are a "safe" person now. Let them see that you are worthy to be trusted and that you are living responsibly, carrying your own load and doing good.

- Your responsibility is to work and take care of your load in life. Don't dump stuff on others. Don't weasel out of things so someone else can take care of it—whether on the job, with family members or with friends.

- Be true to your word and work hard with your abilities, knowing whatsoever you sow, it will come back to you. You are pleasing to God this way.

The Greek tells us that the word burden has two meanings: the "backpack" load and the "boulder" load. The load that refers to one carrying his own backpack in verse 5 is each individual carrying his load of daily responsibilities.

In Galatians 6:2, it says that we are to bear one another's burdens. This is not the backpack load. Paul was telling the Galatians that if they see someone with an overwhelming load or burden that is like a boulder weighing them down, then they need to step in and help them if they can. This would be a crisis situation. Not everything and everyone is in a crisis 24/7. Remember, we don't live in a crisis mode anymore. We are now stable and rooted in Christ, not tossed to and fro as we used to be. We carry our own "backpack load" and are ready to assist those who may be in a real crisis whenever it is in our power to do so.

The worst injustice a parent can do is to enable his child by not making him responsible for his own messes such as cleaning his room, doing chores, keeping up his school grades and working out relationships with others. If we interfere, then one truly doesn't learn life's lessons. For example, a child gets bad grades in school because he never did his homework. Should the parents be up in the face of the school administrator when he says that their child must go to summer school or he won't be able to pass on to the next grade? No! (But I have seen this happen over and over. The parent interferes and so the child doesn't have any true consequences.) Of course, no one wants the inconvenience of it all, but the child needs to suffer the consequences and pay the price. Consequences for actions are a way of life and unless we really learn from them, we will repeat the same mistakes over and over again on into adulthood.

Yes, we can be adults and still be learning the same lessons from childhood. This is what I call repeating the second grade for the fifth time! How silly it would be to see a grown man sitting in the second grade. But how many of us are there in certain areas of our lives? It's time to learn these lessons once and for all and grow up! People in addictions seem to suffer in this area. Another example is a parent who may fear losing his or her child. Maybe he had been abandoned by the other spouse so he keeps that child close by like a "buddy." They hang out, confiding in adult issues, sleep together, and even wear each other's clothes. But this is not a true parent–child relationship. Instead, it is a dysfunctional relationship that occurs because of the parent's own insecurities and fears.

When this happens, when the child is grown, he will often have deep-seated resentment that stems from never learning the proper role of submission to authority. And if that child has any sense in him, he will flee from that parent as fast as he can when he gets older! This child may even drop out of school because he doesn't how to interact with his own peers, since adults had been his only peers. I've seen it happen over and over, where the child feels more comfortable with adults so that he becomes robbed of his own childhood.

When he gets older, it may take the law, military, or others to bring him into submission, because he still hasn't learned one of life's valuable lessons—that someone else is in charge! None of us are ever islands unto ourselves. There will always be someone over us, whether we like it or not. Until we learn this, we will not make good children, students, parents, employees or leaders. We also cannot have a healthy functional life like we desire.

Then there is the parent who controls with his money so his child, even at forty years old is still not functional without daddy or mommy's permission. What a disgrace! When that parent does die, that individual falls apart and doesn't know how to live as a normal adult. He then squanders and wastes all his inheritance through unhealthy relationships of users.

I know firsthand people who embody these three examples that I shared with you. These people in their selfish, worldly love and insecurities actually created dysfunctional children, who in turn will produce more dysfunctional children if the cycle doesn't stop. Look at our society—people are takers and not true givers. They are not giving to society and to the future of their children, the next generation.

Ephesians 4:28 says, "Let him that stole steal no more: but rather let him labour, working with his hands the thing which is good, that he may have to give to him that needeth." Stealing isn't just taking something physical, but it can be an emotional, social, environmental and of course, a spiritual experience. Stealing is not just a physical thing; it is a mindset! But don't steal people's time anymore, you don't waste your time anymore, and you know when to stop things and turn them off—because you have self- control. You are not out of control anymore; you live differently now!

Here's an example that everyone can relate to. When they have free mints at the restaurant, do you stuff a handful in your pocket or just take one? It isn't the candy that is the real issue, as much as it is the attitude of "I can take what I want, they owe me, I paid for it, and they have more than enough." God always looks at our hearts.

It starts with the smallest things. So catch yourself and think about what you are doing. Think about what you are taking—is it really yours to take? Do they really owe you? What would Jesus do? –Ouch, that one hurts!

The Bible says that if we don't work, we don't eat. It tells us not to give what doesn't cost us something. It is easy to give away what one doesn't own or didn't earn. It is easy to take other people's stuff and give it away, but this is wrong! You have no right to reap where you did not sow!

First John 3:17 says, "But whoso hath this world's good, and seeth his brother have need, and shutteth up his bowels of compassion from him, how dwelleth the love of God in him?" Ask God to give you a heart of compassion for others as He has towards you. The more you learn of His love for you, the more you will have His love in you. Is God a cheater? Is God a swindler? Then why are you? If we are not obeying His Word, then we are not dwelling in Him but rather relying on our old ways to get what we want.

We now do those things that are pleasing in His sight. We don't respond to the old methods as we did before. How can we do His will without Him and His love in us? We can't! Without Him, we can do _____ . But with Him and in Him, we can do all things!

Confession

I have the life of God in me. I have his nature and His ability. I have put off the old man and I have put on Christ. I am a doer of the Word of God and not just a hearer only, because that would only be deceiving myself. I walk in the light as He is in the light. I work with my hands. I don't live to use people anymore. I don't live to steal, cheat or swindle. I don't live to get my own way. I live to do God's will for my life. I can do all things through Christ who lives in me and strengthens me.

My former man has passed away and my life is now hid in Christ. I am not the man I used to be. I am a brand new person! I have His thoughts and His ways in me now. People see a real change in me because I am really changed. They see the love of God in me, and it draws them to Christ. I let my light shine now and I don't hide it anymore, in Jesus' name.

> Day #2: Romans 5:5 says that the love of God is shed abroad in my heart by the Holy Spirit so I can be changed on the inside. What is on the inside of me will effect what is on the outside of me! God's love controls my actions now. I am motivated by His love.

1. I am no longer looking to give to validate myself (so I will feel important) because.....

2. I respect the boundaries of others and am not always pushing others' limits because....

3. I am not giving with strings attached (wearing a "you owe me" mentality) because...

4. I reverse the role from being a taker to being a giver because.....

5. I don't manipulate and use like I used to do to get what I want because....

Choose one of these phrases above and finish the rest of it and tell why you wrote it:

_____

_____

_____

_____

_____

_____

_____

_____

_____

_____

_____

_____

_____

_____

_____

_____

_____

_____

_____

Read and write out John 15:5:

_____

_____

_____

_____

_____

God's way is laying down one's life for another. His way says, "I am not thinking about my needs; instead I care for the needs of others first, and then mine will be taken care of—God will make sure of it. This is what a healthy relationship is all about—giving without expecting anything in return. Ephesians 5 talks about us about preferring others, especially in the marriage relationship. We are to show our spouses due benevolence.

Volunteering in the church is another way we can give of ourselves. When you volunteer, ask yourself this question: Am I doing it to be seen by others or am I doing it out of a giving heart or because God told me to do it? Read Matthew 6 and carefully mediate on these verses. If your heart is not right, it will eventually be known by all. For what is hidden, will be revealed.

For example, have you ever seen an angry usher? Why is he even serving in that capacity? His job is to make the churchgoers feel welcome, as well as safe. Is he doing it to be seen of men, as a duty, or to get a good seat? What are his real motives? Do people experience the love of God through this kind of person and his hospitality gifts?

Some of us go overboard in volunteering because we are so excited about God in our lives now and want to serve. But this could also be because of our addictive personality. You must take heed so you don't substitute your addictions for people and get caught up in people addictions. Always search the motives of your heart and ask yourself, "Why am I volunteering? Did God tell me to do it?" I truly believe where God plants you, you will grow. Yet, we can so easily become overcommitted that we break under pressure and end up looking like we're not faithful at all. Then no one will risk depending on our help for any type of leadership position. Know your limitations; don't go overboard! Where He guides, He provides. Giving to God for you, might be giving to Him by spending time on your face in prayer and journaling, crying your heart out to Him to get some answers so a real change can occur in your life. It may not be serving around people at all. And that is okay! Of course, you must go to church and not forsake the assembly of the brethren as it says in Hebrews 10:25. But you can't go around being a people pleaser; you must be a God pleaser!

There will always be work to do in the church. Your job is to find out where you fit. What does God want you to do? That's where you will be content and be anointed to work. He will enable you to do what He has called you to do. There will be a grace that comes on you and you will love doing it. It won't be drudgery or burdensome. If it is, then you need to re-evaluate the situation because maybe you are not in the right place.

People have relapsed because they couldn't handle all of their commitments and they didn't know how to pull back. Therefore, they withdrew and collapsed. Some even use the excuse that they were on a long prayer and fasting vigil just to get some much needed space and rest. But God knows differently! Be honest and just say you got overcommitted and need to pull back. Otherwise, a root of resentment will have an open door to seep in. Some have used this as a good excuse to go back to the old patterns of their old man and say, "I am tired of being a Christian. All I do is give and give and never feel appreciated." Yet, God never told them to do certain things that they feel they must do to validate themselves. When they do this, burnout will result and bitterness can take root if not recognized and dealt with immediately. The trap of Satan has been set, and the bait has been taken when one falls for this! We must guard ourselves and know our limits. We need to know when to say 'yes' and when to say 'no.' It is okay to say 'no,' you know? God has instituted boundaries for our safety and well-being.

Write out what you are involved in (job, sports, church, hobbies, etc.).

_____

_____

_____

_____

_____

What should you not be involved in, even if it is good?

_____

_____

_____

_____

It is much easier when things are categorized as good and bad. But it is a lot harder to differentiate the two when it is good and good. Ask yourself if it is just good or if it is what God wants from you. Just because it is a good thing, doesn't mean it is God's will for you to do it. Only you will really know by spending time with the Father. He will always lead you to do the right thing.

There can be times that you get committed and don't really know that you made the wrong decision until you are deep in the middle of it. Brother Keith Moore always taught us, "If it is not quite, then it is not right!" If you come to this realization, humble yourself and get out of it quickly, as it says in Proverbs. Besides, if you are filling that position, the real person who belongs there can't get in his position. You are out of place and won't receive the blessings, because God is only required to bless you when you are in your place—when you are in His will for your life. It is too costly to not be in the right place at the right time, doing the right thing! A lot of us have learned this the hard way—being in the wrong place at the wrong time, doing the wrong thing. And what a price we paid for it!

When we were using or abusing, we were always pushing the boundaries and did whatever we felt like doing. However, it is not that way anymore. Ephesians 2:8-9 says, "For by grace are ye saved through faith; and that not of yourselves: it is the gift of God: Not of works, lest any man should boast." Salvation is not by works and it will never be by works! You don't have to try and prove something anymore.

It is not your good works and it is not your bad works that move God, it is only the work of Christ that causes Him to move in your life. Thank God for His divine intervention! You now do things out of a true servant's heart—to serve and to please because the love of God is shed abroad in your heart by the Holy Ghost.

It is okay to give of your time, your substance and yourself, but first take time to get strong in the Lord so you won't be bouncing here and there. You need to get stabilized and that isn't going to happen overnight or even in a few months. It will take a while—probably the rest of your life! But when you are established and rooted, you'll have something to give. You will be that tree in Psalm 1 that lets it roots go down deep and lives by the rivers of water, and your fruit won't wither and people will be blessed by your life! You will be happy and at rest in your soul, knowing you are right with God and living your life in His will (Psalm 23). This is not a self-centered attitude as some have claimed, but it is wisdom to get yourself healthy first, then you can be a blessing and have something to give to others.

Confession

I have the mind of Christ. I know my Father's voice and the voice of the stranger I will not follow. I am not driven like before. I am at peace, and I walk in the Spirit and not in the flesh. I use my time wisely. I know what God's will is for my life and I do it. I lay aside all the extra things that would interfere with my time and walk with the Lord. He has anointed me to do His work, not my own works. So this day, I choose to do what He wants me to do. I am led by the inward witness and peace of the Holy Spirit, in Jesus' name.

Day #3: Read Luke 6:27-28, 38 and write out what these verses mean to you:

_____

_____

_____

_____

_____

_____

_____

In the past, we always expected people to do things for us because of our addictions. We had a welfare mentality. So instead of getting up and doing things on our own, we looked for someone we could mooch from or use. We were actually draining the very life out of them, because they were living to give for validation, and we were living to take for dependence purposes. Both parties were caught up in the insanity of a dysfunctional life. Perhaps it was a continuation from childhood and the only way of life that we knew. But it was still not healthy and would prove to be detrimental to our welfare if we continued in it.

Now we are in Christ Jesus and our old man and its past is gone, so we don't put on the works of the flesh anymore. We now walk in the Spirit and fulfill the law of Christ. When we accept Christ, the dysfunctional nature is wiped away from our lives. We have a new life to live now—one that we may not have been familiar with, yet one that promises us everything we had been searching for our entire lives: peace, stability, security, sense of self -worth, a sound mind, love, and the list goes on. But the most important gift we have received is acceptance from our Father God and eternal life through Christ Jesus our Lord—and it starts now living it on this earth!

God gives us a second chance in life, a fresh start. We go out of our way to bless others. We turn the cheek if we have to do so. We give and we do not lend. If we lend, then we are always looking for the "payback." So give if you have it to give and don't, if you don't! God says let your yes be yes and your no be no. Anything else is sin. We have put away indecisiveness. We keep our word now and we don't take it back. We follow through on commitments and promises, no matter what the cost. We give and it is given back to us. God will make sure of it when you are pleasing Him.

Confession

This is the day the Lord has made. I will rejoice and be glad in it. I am not the man I used to be. I am faithful. I keep my word. I give because I love to give. My Father God is a giver so I am a giver. I will give when it is in my power to do so. I will keep my word so I may bring glory to the Lord's name. I am reliable. I have a stable life now. I do not quit and run away, but I persevere to the end. Christ is in me and I am in Him. This life that I live, I now live in Christ Jesus. I am not my own, I have been bought with the blood of God's dear Son. He first gave to me and now I give my all to Him. In Jesus' name, I pray.

Read and write out in the Amplified version, I Corinthians 13: 4-8. It would be good to memorize these scriptures and make them a personal confession for yourself.

_____

_____

_____

_____

_____

_____

_____

_____

_____

_____

_____

_____

_____

_____

_____

_____

_____

_____

Day #4: A myth: co-dependent people do not have addictions. This is not true! They are addicted to controlling the person with addictions, therefore they are addicted to a dysfunctional lifestyle as well! In fact, some codependents go out of their way to rescue someone in need of their good graces. However, they don't realize that have just invited the devil to come and move in with them. The world separates the co-dependent and the alcoholic, but God does not. Sin is sin, regardless of the category it is in.

If it is not of God, it is sin! And this may shock some, but if you have the addictive personality—you are the addict or alcoholic—you are also co-dependent because you are addicted to an abnormal lifestyle. Which sad to say, has become the norm in our society: everyone functioning dysfunctionally! Only in the Word of God can we find out who we really are and function the way God meant for us to live.

I truly believe the person labeled as co-dependent actually has more issues to deal with than the addict. They are like the righteous brother of the prodigal son who we read about in Luke 15, because they think they are so right and holy because of their good deeds. But when the addict, like the prodigal, gets delivered, he really repents! He is so set free, so he can a lot of times easily let go of the past and press on because he knows how detrimental it is if he doesn't let it go. But the co-dependent person never wants you to forget.

A lot of times, the co-dependent isn't happy about the addict's newfound freedom, so they want to continually remind him of the past and hold him in a state of "guilty" limbo. They are still full of the bitterness, hurts and disappointments caused by the "set free" addict and they don't want them to forget it! They refuse to respect boundaries as well and they continue to live with a "You owe me" mentality. All this is very dysfunctional! If they are to have any hope of restoration in the future, both parties must let go of the past and allow God to heal them We must hear people's 'yes" and 'no's' and not push our will onto others. God never pushes His will onto us. If He did, He would make us all get saved!

Examples of Breaking or Setting Boundaries

- When dating, if a guy doesn't hear the word "no", he is a boundary breaker

- Saying "no" to someone you care about because they are bringing a destructive lifestyle into the home around the family is establishing a healthy boundary

- Booting the young adult out of the house and telling him to get a job if it is time for him to leave. This is also setting healthy boundaries and forcing one to grow up and take ownership of his responsibilities and actions.

A new mindset must occur in the former addict: "I will sink or swim and I will not run away; I will not give in under pressure; I will not freak out and use again."

You must hold on to your Father God and endure. If you do, you will make it through and become stronger than before. You won't chuck the job after a few weeks nor will you tell people sob stories so they will bail you out, but you will become an honest individual, working with your own hands and carrying your own burden in society. You will lift your head high when you do this. Things will change as long as you don't quit, give in, or give up! You won't run away anymore when the going gets tough—and it will get tough before it gets better! Are you ready?

The enemy knows your weaknesses and he is going to push and push, but you must push back and take a stand, resist him, and tell him where to go. Besides, where else are you going to go now that you have the words of life and know the truth? Are you going to return back to the vomit again? Proverbs 26:11 says, "As a dog returneth to his vomit, so a fool returneth to his folly." Our first boundary word ever was "No!" 'No' is not always a bad thing. You need to say 'no' to the devil, 'no' to someone who is going to hurt you, 'no' to taking drugs, 'no' to taking away from your family, and 'no' to drinking because it leads to death. Reverse the scenario. If you were a taker, now be the giver, if you were the giver, codependent, now be the taker and believe and receive by faith. Allow others to have self-dignity.

Many years ago after I had already moved away from home, President Reagan put some new laws in place and my mom had to go to work for the first time at 45 years old! She was so upset at first, because she had taken care of us through living off of the welfare system for several decades. But it was the best thing for her to get out of that dependent cycle. It restored her self-worth again, and also gave her a pension to retire on. God is always looking out for us— for our future—even when we don't think there is a better way. He has a better way!

Matthew 6:33 says, "But seek ye first the kingdom of God, and his righteousness; and all these things shall be added unto you." If He gives it to you, you're not going to lose it! God provides where He guides. If He tells you to go to Bible school, then He is obligated to take care of you. If He tells you to take a lesser job, then He will make up the difference.

The important thing is to obey what He tells you to do. Pastor Kenneth W. Hagin preached a sermon called, A Place Called There. (I highly recommend that everyone listen to this CD.) You will never have lack in the place that is your "there." Just make sure you're there!

Read Mark 4:21-25 and write out what it means to you:

_____

_____

_____

_____

_____

_____

_____

Confession

I seek first the kingdom of God and His righteousness and all these things—things I want, things I need, will be added unto me. God promises me that as I put Him first, He will give me the desires of my heart. He will bless me as I live for Him. I don't have to worry or fret like the world does. God takes good care of His kids. I am His child and God takes good care of me.

I will do my part and work hard and I trust Him to do His part and provide. I am on the side of the law and not against it anymore. I am honest and I work with my hands. I respect others and don't push my way or wants on them. I am a new creation in Christ Jesus now. I don't run when things get hard. I don't try to get others to carry my load. I call upon my Heavenly Father and He gives me strength to carry on. I can do all things because of Him now living on the inside of me. Amen.

> Day #5: Read Matthew 5:38-48. God doesn't want us to react the old way anymore. He wants us to live in and act like Christ. Matthew 5:1-12 is called the Beatitudes of Christ, the attitudes of Christ. This is how He wants us to act now. In these verses, we can actually see how God wants us to "be." Take time to read these verses. Write what you have learned from these verses:

_____

_____

_____

_____

_____

_____

_____

_____

_____

God tells us to love our enemies. Now that can be a hard thing to do, especially if we always live to pay back! But the love of God that is now abiding on the inside of us does not want us to retaliate. I don't know about you, but that has been hard for me at times. However, the things I like to stress is just because you are a Christian, doesn't mean that you are a doormat. God doesn't want us to be used or taken advantage of, but I think because we came out of that, that will be the last thing we would ever allow to happen to us. But we have to watch ourselves so we don't do that to others. We don't want to bulldoze over people because we are on this mission now of sanctification in Christ. It is a good thing to feel passionate about Christ, but it's not a good thing to run over other believers or weak-willed individuals.

We need to be quick to forgive and give others the benefit of the doubt. We should believe the best of people just like we would want them to believe the best of us. God doesn't want us to act unmannerly or rude. We have put off our old ways and put on Christ. It's like taking off dirty old clothing and putting on nice clean clothes. When people see God's love in us and what God has delivered us from, it will cause them to take notice and they will be drawn to the Lord by our testimony.

The love of God is what leads men to repentance, a change of mind and of heart. It is not looking down on people or treating them rudely that will win their hearts. Condemnation never works; it only drives a person further away from the truth.

Write out what areas you still need to put off and what you can put on in place of these things. Christianity is the great exchange. We exchange our filthy rags for His robe of righteousness.

Write out 1 Peter 4:1-2:

_____

_____

_____

_____

_____

_____

_____

Confession

I have the mind of Christ, and I have put on His attitudes now. I put on love and choose to believe the best of every person and every situation. I will not lose my cool, because I am quick to forgive and forget. I move on. I don't take time to judge others, because I am too busy judging myself. I don't have time to hold grudges. I take the beam out of my own eye first.

I give and it is given unto me. I sow love, therefore I receive love. I sow peace and I reap peace. I walk away from strife. Those who cause strife have no part in my circle. I am known by my fruit and my fruit is good and brings glory to God, because I am a child of God. My Heavenly Father loves me and that is all that matters!

I live this day to please Him and He causes even my worst enemy to be at peace with me. He causes my worst situation to work out somehow. I don't strive in the flesh anymore and do things through sheer willpower, but instead I walk in the Spirit of God. I have His wisdom and discernment in me and I am not deceived anymore. Amen.

Day #6: Read John 10:1-18. Write what this passage is talking about:

_____

_____

_____

_____

_____

_____

_____

_____

_____

_____

_____

_____

_____

The thief is always looking for another way in the door, instead of the right way. We are children of God now. We do not function and operate like we have in the past. The father of all lies is Satan. He is the true thief. John 10:10 says, "The thief cometh not, but for to steal, and to kill, and to destroy: I am come that they might have life, and that they might have it more abundantly." The devil tries to sneak in any way he can. He hates us because we are made in the image and likeness of God. That's why he wants to destroy us. But Christ has come that we might have abundant life.

God is the giver and the devil is the taker. God always wants to make us whole and restore things back to us. He is not the one who destroys or puts sickness on us. The best way to look at it is that anything good comes from God, and anything bad comes from Satan. James 1:17 says, "Every good gift and every perfect gift is from above, and cometh down from the Father of lights, with whom is no variableness, neither shadow of turning."

Write out the good things that you know God has given you:

_____

_____

_____

_____

_____

_____

_____

Confession

I know the voice of the Good Shepherd. I follow His Word. I am a doer of the Word of God. Christ has come to give me life and in Him is no darkness at all. I have no darkness in me because the Anointed One abides on the inside of me. He anoints me to live in Him. He has given me life and life more abundantly. Anything good that happens in my life today is from my Father and anything bad that tries to come my way is not from the Lord.

I resist you Satan and command you to desist in your works against me and my family. No weapon formed against me will prosper—in word or deed. I am a doer of the Word of God and I am blessed in my deeds. All my needs are met, in Jesus' name. Amen.

Day #7: Find four scriptures about the love of Christ or giving and write them out:

_____

_____

_____

_____

_____

_____

_____

_____

_____

_____

_____

_____

_____

_____

_____

_____

Proverbs 10:12 says, "Love covereth all sins." God has covered my sins by the blood of His dear Son, Jesus. His love covers me now. John 3:16 says so! No one can take that away from me. Now that I know how much God loves me, I am able to press on to my destiny. No more destructive living for me, because He has set me free from the tyranny of the enemy! Hallelujah!

Confession

I walk in the spirit and not in the flesh. The love of God compels me to do good works. I bring glory to His name with my life. My life is not my own now for it is hid in Christ. The life that I now live, I live by the faith of the Son of God who loved me and gave Himself for me. He loves me and cares for me. I love and care for others. I am not self-seeking. I am loving and kind. I am full of patience and self-control.

Nothing or no one controls me anymore. The flesh cannot dominate me. I recognize the enemy's tactics and I don't fall for them anymore. My feelings are not in control of my life. My spirit man has full reign now. I am spirit-led and Word fed. I live and move and have my being in Christ. I confess and meditate on the Word of God, because it has the power within it to save my soul and to deliver me from all sin. Amen.

NOTES

_____

_____

_____

_____

_____

_____

_____

_____

_____

_____

_____

_____

_____

_____

CONFESSIONS

Milestone Confessions #1

- Jesus is Lord over my spirit, soul, and body. I belong to Him now. I am not my own for I have been bought with a price, the blood of Christ. (1 Peter 1:18-19)

- The Lord is my shepherd. I do not want. I do not want anything that is harmful to my body. My God supplies all my needs according to His riches in glory in Christ Jesus. I have control of my life now. (Psalms 23:1-2, Philippians 4:19)

- I do not fret. I am not anxious about anything. I do not have a care because I refuse to worry. I have cast all my cares upon the Lord, for He cares for me. I don't give in to triggers like before. When I get anxious, I am reminded to call on God instead of running to addictive behaviors because I am addicted to Christ now! (Philippians 4:6, 1 Peter 5:6-7)

- I have the mind of Christ and have His thoughts, feelings and purposes of His heart. He puts His desires in my heart. So I can say God does give me the desires of my heart! And I crave and hunger for the things of God and not the things of this world. (1 Corinthians 2:16, Psalms 37:4)

- I let the words of Christ dwell in me richly. I know that He who began a good work in me will continue it until the day of Christ. (Colossians 3:16, Philippians1:6)

- I am no longer afraid, for God has not given me a spirit of fear. Instead, He has given me a spirit of power to overcome.

He has given me a spirit of love to receive and give love again. He has given me a sound mind. I am no longer tormented with bad thoughts. I can think clearly now for I have a sober mind. (2 Timothy 1:7, Romans 12:3, 1 Peter 1:13, 1 Peter 5:8)

- I hear my Father's voice and the voice of strangers I will not follow. I hear the voice of the Good Shepherd and His voice only will I follow. I praise and worship my Father God through songs and psalms, for this silences the enemy's voice. I choose to praise all day long! Hallelujah! Glory to God! (John 10:27, Psalm 8:2)

Milestone Confessions #2

- I can do all things through Christ who strengthens me. I am strong in the Lord and able to say no to anything or anyone that is not good for me. I have a hedge of thorns around me that keeps out unclean and unhealthy relationships. I have discernment and I am not deceived. I hang with wise people and therefore, I am wise. I make wise choices now. I have put away foolishness and put on God's wisdom. (Philippians 4:13, Job 1:10, Ephesians 1:18, Proverbs 13:20)

- I am free from condemnation, for God loves me and has forgiven me. He doesn't condemn me, so I will not condemn myself. I command all condemning voices to be silent right now and I will not yield to them anymore in Jesus' name. (Romans 8:1-2, John 3:17)

- I am free from any and all condemning charges brought against me. God will work everything out for my good because I live for Him. No weapon formed against me shall prosper for I am the righteousness of God in Christ Jesus. (Romans 8:31-

34, Psalm 138:8, Isaiah 54:17)

- I cannot be separated from the love of God. No situation or circumstance can separate me from God's love. I will not separate myself from God's love anymore. (Romans 8:35-39)

- I am born of God and the evil one cannot touch me; I am in God's hands. (1 John 5:18)

- My life is hidden with Christ in God. He is my hiding place. The Lord is my light and my salvation, of whom shall I be afraid? What shall I fear? (Colossians 3:3, Psalm 27:1, Psalm 119:114)

- If my father and mother forsake me, or any other family member rejects me, the Lord will take me up for He is my Heavenly Father. I belong to the family of God. I am not alone or afraid anymore, for I have been made accepted in the beloved. If God accepts me, then I will not be concerned with those who reject me. (Psalm 27:10, Ephesians 1:6)

Milestones Confessions #3

- I am God's child. I have been adopted into the family of God. I have been bought with a price, I belong to Him now. (John 1:12, Ephesians 1:5, 1 Corinthians 6:19-20)

- I am not alone. God is with me and said He would never, never, never, leave me nor forsake me. I don't have to face life alone! He is with me until the end. (Hebrew 13:5)

- I am a member of Christ's body. I am united with the Lord now and I am one spirit with Him. I am in Him and He is in me. (1 Corinthians 12:27, 1 Corinthians 6:17)

- I have been bought with a price, the blood of Jesus Christ. I belong to Him now. I am not my own. I have been crucified with Christ, nevertheless I live, yet not I, but Christ lives in me. And this life that I now live, I live by the faith of the Son of God, who loved me and gave Himself for me. (1 Corinthians 6:19-20, Galatians 2:20)

- I have been redeemed. I am forgiven of all my sins. I can boldly come to God's throne without the sense of inferiority, guilt or condemnation. I now approach Him with freedom and confidence that He hears me and that He cares for me. I am a friend of God. (Colossians 1:14, Ephesians 3:12, John 15:15, Hebrews 4:16)

- I am complete in Christ. The work that Christ has done is sufficient. I cannot earn salvation or work for it. I accept by faith what Christ has done for me. It is by grace that I have been saved and that is a gift from God. (Colossians 2:10, Ephesians 2:8-9)

- I set my affections on things above and not on the things of this earth anymore. I am no longer a friend of this world, but I am a citizen of heaven. My life is hidden in Christ Jesus. (Colossians 3:1-2)

- I get high on the Most High now. I fill myself up with the Holy Spirit of God and get drunk on the new wine. He is all I need! (Ephesians 5:18)

Milestones Confessions #4

- I am God's temple. The Holy Spirit of God resides on the inside of me. I am filled to overflowing with the Holy Ghost. I speak in tongues daily, knowing that I am building myself up every time I do so. (1 Corinthians 3:16, I Corinthians 14:18, Jude 20)

- I have been chosen and appointed to bear fruit. I walk in the Spirit and not in the flesh. I have the fruit of the Spirit working in me. (John 15:16, Galatians 5:16, 22-23)

- The love of God is shed abroad in my heart by the Holy Spirit and His love abides in me richly. I love as God loves. I have put off the works of the flesh and I have put on Christ's love. I choose to walk in love. (Romans 5:5, Colossians 3:9-10)

- I walk in the light as He is in the light and the wicked one touches me not. Greater is He who is in me than He that is in the world. (1 John 5:18, 1 John 4:4)

- I am a new creation in Christ Jesus, old things are passed away and all things have become new in my life. I have a new life. I have a second chance because of Christ! (2 Corinthians 5:17)

- I tread upon serpents, scorpions and over all the power of the enemy and nothing shall harm me. I take the shield of faith, which is the Word of God, and I quench every fiery dart of the wicked one. I am not ignorant of Satan's devices. I don't fall for the old tricks of the enemy anymore. (Psalm 91:13, Ephesians 6:16, Luke 10:19)

- I am born of God and therefore I have overcome the world, the devil and the flesh. I am delivered from the evil of this present world. The law of the spirit in Christ Jesus has made me free from the law of sin and death. I have chosen Christ, therefore, I have chosen life. I choose to live a long productive life in Christ. No more wasted years for me! (1 John 5:4-5, Romans 8:2, John 10:10)

Milestones Confession #5

- I am a believer and not a doubter. I hold fast to the confession of my faith. Faith comes by hearing the Word of God. I choose to hear God's Word daily to grow strong in Christ. I hear His Word and hide it in my heart so that I will not sin against Him. I will not draw back from God for He is my life now. (Hebrews 10:35, Romans 10:17, Psalm 66:18)

- I am quick to repent. I am quick to forgive and slow to get angry; for the wrath of man does not promote the righteousness of God. Therefore, I have put off wrath, malice and anger and I have put on Christ and I now walk in the love of God. (James 1:19-20)

- No weapon formed against me will prosper, for I am the righteousness of God in Christ Jesus. I am planted by the rivers of water like a tree with its roots deep down in the rich soil. I allow my roots to get established in Christ and then I am strong and not so easily swayed. (Isaiah 54:17, Psalm 1:3, Ephesians 3:17)

- Jesus has set me free and if the Son has set me free, I am free indeed! I am free indeed. No more bondage for me! Hallelujah! (John 8:32, Romans 8:15)

- I am assured that all things work together for my good. I am confident that the good work that God has begun in me will be completed. God is ever working in me and will continue until the day Christ returns. I am God's workmanship. He has a plan for my life, a hope and a future for me. He is my future. (Romans 8:28, Philippians 1:6, Ephesians 2:10, Jeremiah 29:11)

- My mind is being transformed daily. It is being renewed by the Word of God and I have offered up my body as a living sacrifice to live the rest of my days for Christ. He is in me and I am in Him. I am not my own anymore. I am the temple of God now. He abides in me and I abide in Him. (Romans 12:1-2, 1 Corinthians 3:16, John 15:4)

Milestones Confessions #6

- I submit myself to God and I resist Satan and he must flee from me. He flees from me in terror when I speak the name of Jesus, for every knee shall bow at the name of Jesus. Every creature in the earth, above the earth and under the earth must bow to Jesus Christ for He is the Lord of lords and the King of kings. (James 4:7, Philippians 2:10-11)

- Whatsoever I bind on this earth is already bound in heaven, and whatsoever I loose on this earth is already loosed in heaven. Therefore in the name of Jesus, I bind all principalities, powers, rulers of darkness and all demoniac forces from operating in my life. I command them to depart from me and do not return in Jesus' name. I belong to Christ now. I am blood bought, therefore I am God's property now! (Matthew 18:18-20, Ephesians 1:19-23)

- I honor God with my body now. I bring glory to His name in all that I do. I have been redeemed from the curse of the law. Sin, sickness, disease and addictions have no control over me. I forbid them to in Jesus' name. Jesus has healed me and delivered me. He has set me free. I am healed by the stripes of Jesus Christ. Healing is God's will for my life and I receive it now! I command my body to be healed and come in line with the Word of God and to function normally the way God created it to work, in Jesus name. (Galatians 3:13, Matthew 8:17, 1 Peter 2:24, 1Corinthians 6:20)

- Your Word is a lamp unto my feet, and a light unto my path. I see and know my way for you Lord are my light and my salvation. (Psalm 119:105, 1 John 1:7, Psalm 27:1)

- You have ordained me to praise, for it silences the enemy. It silences the negative thoughts in my mind. I have a new song in my heart and I will sing it all day long. I will not let the enemy silence my praises! I will not be quiet! I have something to say and to praise my Lord Jesus Christ all the day long. Hallelujah! (Psalm 8:2, Psalm 40:3)

- I am the righteousness of God in Christ Jesus. The life that I now live, I live by faith in the Son of God who loved me and gave Himself for me. Jesus is Lord! (Galatians 2:20)

Milestones Confession #7

- This is the day that the Lord has made. I will rejoice in it and be glad. The joy of the Lord is my strength. No longer am I weak and afraid, but I am strong in the Lord. I am strong to do all things that are healthy and good for me. (Psalm 118:25, Nehemiah 8:10)

- When I praise God, the Lord sets up ambushes against the enemy. Evil can't touch me. (2 Chronicles 20:22)

The wicked one can't touch me. He can't take me out of God's hands. I am blessed. I am protected. God is my shield and buckler and no good thing will He withhold from me because I walk uprightly. (Psalms 91:4, Ephesians 6:16, Psalms 84:11)

- In the midnight hour I will sing praises to my God. I refuse to let the storms of life get on the inside of me. I push back the darkness with my words of praise and thanksgiving. I rejoice and again I say I will rejoice in the Lord. (Acts 16:25, Philippians 4:4)

- The prayers of a righteous man availeth much, making tremendous power available for me. When I pray, things change in my life. I am full of God's power. When I have done all to stand, I will still be standing! (James 5:16, 2 Timothy 1:7, Ephesians 6:10)

- I get drunk on the new wine now. I don't need this world's intoxication! I am filled with the Holy Spirit and His power. That is the only high I will ever need, because there is no high like the Most High! (Ephesians 5:18-20, Acts 1:8)

- He daily loads me with benefits. I am healed. I am delivered from the powers of darkness. I am happy. I am joyful and peaceful. I am full of the fruit of the Spirit and I bear good fruit for His glory. (Psalm 103:1-3, Galatians 5:22-25, Ephesians 1:17-23)

- I have put on Christ and I have put off the flesh. I have put on His robe of righteousness and taken off the filthy garments of this world. I bathe myself in His holy presence. I love to dwell in His presence. I love to dwell in the house of the Lord and with the saints of God. They are my family now. He is my Father. (Colossians 3:10-12, Isaiah 61:10, Psalm 27:4)

- He has delivered me from the power of darkness, translating me into the kingdom of His dear Son, the kingdom of light. I refuse to participate in the works of darkness anymore for I am now a child of the light. I walk in the light as He is in the light. The eyes of my understanding have been enlightened. (Colossians 1:13, Ephesians 2:1-5, 1:18)

- I choose life and not death. I am the head and not the tail, I am above and not beneath. He has blessed me with all spiritual blessings in Christ Jesus. I am like a tree that is planted by the rivers of water. My roots go down deep into God's Word. I cannot be tossed to and fro anymore for I am now firmly planted in Him. (Deuteronomy 28:1-14, 30:19, Psalm 1:3; Ephesians 4:14)

- I delight myself in the Lord and He gives me the desires of my heart. I lean not unto my own understanding but I trust in Him. I rest in Him. (Psalm 37: 3-7, Proverbs 3:5-7)

- It is God's good pleasure to give me the kingdom. He delights in the prosperity of His servants. All good things come from above and all things that are not good do not come from God. God gives life and not death. He gives health and not sickness. He gives wealth and not poverty. He gives me soundness of mind and not confusion. He gives me peace and not strife. He is light and there is no darkness in Him at all. I do not dwell in darkness anymore. I do not fear the future for He is my future. (Psalm 35:17, James 1:17, Galatians 3:14, Colossians 1:13)

- God's Word is my hiding place. I immerse myself in Him. His Word is truth. I hunger and seek truth with all my heart. I put off the works of the flesh and I flee all youthful lusts in Jesus name. I have put on the mind of Christ. (Psalm 32:7, Galatians 5:19, 1 Corinthians 2:16)

- The Lord is good and His mercies endure forever. The Lord is good to me. If I mess up, I fess up and then I get up! The Lord is gracious to me and He loves me. I am quick to make it right when I slip. I won't stay in the pit, but instead will call upon the Lord. He pulls me up and out He sets my feet on solid ground. I get as many chances as I need to get it right, for God will never give up on me! (Psalm 136:1-2, 1 John 1:9, Isaiah 41:10, Psalm 40:1-3)

QUESTIONNAIRE

Alcohol Questionnaire

1. Do you find yourself drinking heavily after a disappointment or a disagreement with someone important to you?

2. When you have trouble or feel pressured, do you drink more than usual?

3. Have you noticed you can handle more liquor than you did when you first began?

4. Do you ever wake up after a night of drinking and cannot remember the night before, even though your friends try to convince you that you didn't pass out?

5. When drinking with people, do you sneak more drinks at gatherings without others knowing?

6. Are there occasions that you feel uncomfortable because no alcohol is around?

7. Have you noticed being in a hurry compared to how you used to be to get that first drink?

8. Do you ever feel guilty about your drinking?

9. Do you secretly get mad when you hear family and friends discuss your drinking?

10. Has there been an increase in memory black-outs?

11. Do you ever want to continue on drinking, even when your friends say they have had enough?

12. Do you usually give a good excuse for the occasion since you drank too much?

13. When you are sober, do you often regret what you said or did while drinking?

14. Have you switched brands or other kinds of alcohol beverages to try and control your drinking?

15. Have you failed on your resolutions of cutting back or quitting alcohol?

16. Have you ever tried to control your drinking by switching jobs or moving to a new location?

17. Do you try to avoid family or close friends while you drink?

18. Are you having an increase in financial or work-related problems?

19. Do more people seem to be treating you unfairly without good reason?

20. Do you eat very little or irregularly when you are drinking?

21. Do you have shakes in the morning and find out it helps to have a little drink?

22. Have you recently noticed that you cannot drink as you once did?

23. Do you sometimes stay drunk for several days at a time?

24. Do you sometimes feel very depressed and wonder whether life is worth living?

25. After periods of drinking, do you see or hear things that are not there?

26. Do you get terribly frightened after you have been drinking heavily?

If you have answered yes to any of these questions, you have some symptoms that may indicate problem drinking. "Yes" answers to the questions indicate the following stages:

Questions 1-8 = Problem Drinking Stage

Questions 9-21= Dependency Drinking Stage

Questions 22-26= Addiction Drinking Stage

Are You Co-Dependent?

1. I can't stand to be alone.

2. I am a perfectionist.

3. I am driven by the approval of others.

4. I find myself making decisions based on how they affect other people and rarely consider myself.

5. Many times I feel obsessed by a need for total order in my life.

6. I put work first above anything.

7. I do not experience anger.

8. I find myself overeating quite often.

9. I am constantly wondering what other people think of me.

10. I find myself adjusting to my spouse's needs rather than communicating my feelings.

11. I have a tendency to cover up my feelings so others won't know what I am really thinking.

12. I am afraid that if others really knew me, they would run and hide.

13. I am constantly trying to figure out how to stay ahead in my relationships.

14. I cover up feelings of self-doubt with drug or alcohol use.

15. I can't say no when I am asked to do a favor or serve on a committee.

16. When I begin to feel sad or angry, I go shopping, work harder or eat.

17. I feel desperate when I can't gain the approval of other people.

18. I tell myself it shouldn't hurt so much when others let me down.

19. I need to control those close to me.

20. I need everyone to be happy with me so that I can feel good about myself.

21. I need others to be strong for me without requiring anything from me in return.

If you checked two or more of the preceding statements, you have some codependent issues. You are a human being, created in God's image. Be careful about labeling yourself as a co-dependent in an unhealthy way. Instead, use the label to face the unhealthy behaviors going on in your life. Don't use it to shame yourself. Each person has been through a set of unique experiences that have led to these problems of feelings of hopelessness and unhealthy behavior.

- From Love is a Choice workbook, authors: Dr. Heifelt, Minirth, Meirer D. Newman, and B. Newman

Safe vs. Unsafe People

1. Unsafe: Unstable over time

2. Safe: Consistent and reliable over time

3. Unsafe: Believe they are perfect and have no faults

4. Safe: Admit they have faults, and try to work on them

5. Unsafe: Condemn and cut it off with others when they get offended

6. Safe: Forgive others and stay connected

7. Unsafe: Avoid closeness with others

8. Safe: Are able to connect to others

9. Unsafe: Lie instead of telling the truth

10. Safe: Tell the truth and face the consequences

11. Unsafe: A negative influence

12. Safe: A positive influence

13. Unsafe: Are stagnant

14. Safe: Are growing

15. Unsafe: Only apologizes

16. Safe: Apologizes and changes behaviors

17. Unsafe: Demands trust

18. Safe: Earns trust over time

19. Unsafe: Self-righteous

20. Safe: Humble and teachable

21. Unsafe: Religious

22. Safe: Spiritual

23. Unsafe: Defensive

24. Safe: Open to feedback

25. Unsafe: Avoids working on their problems

26. Safe: Deals with problems, wants to change

27. Unsafe: Are only concerned with "I"

28. Safe: Concerned with "we"

29. Unsafe: Gossips and tells secrets

30. Safe: Keeps secrets

31. Unsafe: Blames others instead of taking responsibility

32. Safe: Takes responsibility for their actions – right or wrong

33. Unsafe: Think they have it all together and don't admit their faults

34. Safe: Does admit their weaknesses

35. Unsafe: Stays in parent / child roles instead of relating as equals

36. Safe: Understands and is willing to relate as equals

37. Unsafe: Doesn't hear your "no"

38. Safe: Respects your "no"

39. Unsafe: Doesn't understand nor respect your privacy

40. Safe: Gives you space, understands your need for alone time

Use this to compare the relationship you are in right now. If you circled more unsafe than safe comments, you are most likely in an unsafe relationship and need to get some help. Assess yourself first to make sure you are a safe person, then do the same for the other person. Do this periodically to see how you have grown or if you find yourself back in the same kind of relationship as before.

- Information and ideas gleaned and compiled from Safe People / Dr. Cloud, Dr. Townsend

Milestones: Unhealthy Boundaries

- You feel like you are in a parent-child relationship with you being the parent.

- You are exhausted all the time, but don't feel like you have time to rest because you are too busy day and night. You have too much to do. You make impossible lists.

- You have difficulty sleeping and don't get proper rest.

- You do not have time for genuine friendships or relationships, even though you long for them. You don't know how to connect.

- There is no joy in your life; everything seems so difficult. You are negative about the future and find yourself complaining more and more.

- You overindulge in foods such as sweets, coffee, sodas, etc. These are your comfort foods or your reward for yourself.

- It seems you do not have happy memories.

- You dread your day before it begins.

- You find yourself always dealing with crisis or people who are in crisis, not knowing how to say no to them or avoid getting in the crisis in the first place.

- You are the giver and not in a "give and take" healthy relationship.

- You seem to be working harder to keep the peace, but it is only getting worse.

- You do things for others when you really want to say "no" which causes resentment.

- You feel very lonely and isolated and don't know how to change it.

- You are always taking the blame for others' faults and dysfunctions.

- You never relax or take time for yourself.

- You can't separate from unhealthy people because of fear or resentment. You feel obligated to connect with them even though they are not good for you.

- You do not keep up with your personal hygiene. You do not feel good about yourself.

- You find yourself trying to fix other people, not allowing them to take ownership of their own responsibilities.

Write out and discuss one or two of these in your group and be honest and open about sharing what you know is true about you. Then ask for help for how to change and most of all, ask for prayer. _____

_____

_____

_____

_____

_____

_____

_____

_____

CHURCH INVOLVEMENT AND COMMUNITY OUTREACH

We believe in this day and age, every church must have a recovery program. It needs to be as important as any other outreach program, if not more so. Alcohol, drugs and sexual addictions are rampant in our society and in the church. Many don't want to address it or admit it. Nevertheless, these issues are of epidemic proportions among Christians. Even Bible colleges and schools are not exempt. One cannot assume because someone goes to church or Bible school that they are cured and have no more problems in these areas.

If the church doesn't provide help and tries to ignore it, addictions in the church will only become worse. Some churches try to ignore people with addiction issues until they go away and leave. Others just tolerate them and try to keep it silent and still use them as volunteers in the church, but don't really reach out and help them. These people who desperately need help will get so burned out and go elsewhere or sad to say, will fall away from the Lord due to shame and guilt and a "no way out" feeling of hopelessness.

We are to help, give hope and to provide healing to a hurting world, especially our church world. A minister once said it well, "A church is like a hospital; it is where you go to get healed." There will be people at all levels of growth at church. The church must not be ashamed to talk about it from the pulpit or let the people know that there is a place that they provide to help them.

If you ask pastors what are the top problems in counseling, sexual and chemical addictions will most likely be mentioned, along with money problems that most likely stemmed from the addictions. There is a great book called When Addictions Come to Church by Melinda Fish. I highly recommend that all outreach ministers and pastors read it. It is possible that your usher, greeter, prayer worker, Sunday school teacher or choir member may be secretly dealing with some sort of addiction but are afraid to seek help because of the fear of banishment, rejection or even church persecution.

The pastor of the church needs to let people know that addictions are sin like any other sin and Jesus died on the cross for them as well. One can be set free, it just needs to be dealt with and not kept secret. If the pastor goes a step further and offers help, many more people will be in church instead of watching church on television and wishing they could be there. Jesus doesn't condemn us. Instead He provided a way for us to be free and we are to do the same! We are His hands, His feet and His body, remember?

Get involved with the community. Let the police stations, courthouses and judges know you have an alternate Christian recovery program and want to work with them. Most of them will thank you for it and will send people your way. Take your drug program to the county jails and prisons or establish a local coffee shop to have addiction recovery meetings there. Promote it as you would a feeding the homeless or prison outreach, then maybe they will never get to that point!

SOME GUIDELINES FOR STARTING A PROGRAM

The Vision / Mission Statement

Everyone needs a vision. One must be able to see it to follow after it. It should be scripturally based. Ask the Lord to give you a fresh revelation of what He wants for your people. In Habakkuk 2 it says to write the vision down, make it plain, or understandable, so the people who read it can also see it and run with it. People have to know what they are pursuing and need constant reminders.

Groups

Age Limit: 17 years and older / No children!

Always separate the men from the women. They will open up and talk more freely if you do. If the group gets too large (more than 14), separate the codependents from the addicts in both the men's and women's groups. You need to deal with the addiction issues before you can get into the boundary problems but all addicts have them! I want to stress that you don't have to do it this way, just follow the guideance of the Holy Spirit for the needs of the people God has called you to reach.

Leaders and Workers

All workers must be approved members and volunteers of the church first. Then they need to be approved by the recovery program leaders. They also should be required to go through the 12 Milestones sessions before they take any leadership position. We feel that the leaders, or at least the main leader of the program, must have had past experience in addictions personally. That way they will be able to understand the issues that will arise and the attendees will feel that they truly can relate to someone who has been in their shoes.

Curriculum

Use the Milestones! Everyone needs to have their own Milestone book and a Bible. They need to follow along in the Milestones book and write in it, using it as an interactive journal and doing the homework that will be reviewed next week in the circles. Follow the Milestones and do a 12 week cycle program. Anyone can come in at any time since it is a continuous program. Some will just come to obey the court order and obtain an attendance certificate. But people may want to stay at the program for a year or more. Don't discourage this, for recovery is different for everyone! Sell the books at the program too, so they can be obtained easily. Don't feel bad about selling the books because when things are purchased, they are usually appreciated much more and it is important for the individual to be investing in his or her own recovery. Besides, it will be a lot less than what the addiction will cost!

Importance of Literature

We strongly believe in placing literature into people's hands. Knowledge is powerful. A person must first know before he can do. My husband was saved after reading a tract left in a public restroom. I was saved through reading a book that was passed around in the county jail. We know the importance of getting as much as you can into a person's hands, for it may be the only chance and opportunity for some. We don't get discouraged if a person only makes it to a program one time as long as we can load them up with "free literature." People who are serious about change will read and reread the material when they get alone. And you have sown some seed!

Childcare

I believe that every program should provide childcare if you have the facilities to do it. Start off from the very beginning offering these services. We recommend you use the church's volunteers who have already been screened, trained and approved to work in the Children's Department. It would be good to pay your workers if your budget allows it, or expect the parents to pay a small nominal fee per child. This way you will get good quality workers and there will be consistency.

Transportation

If you have the means, such as a church bus or van, and have a licensed driver who would be willing to drive attendees back and forth then this can be a blessing for those who could not attend otherwise. (Check the laws where you live to find out if your driver needs a special license, etc.) It is best to never use your own personal vehicles and workers should not ever get personally involved or take attendees anywhere in their own vehicles and definitely not the opposite sex! There are those who have lost their driver's license, those who can't drive, and even groups from rehabs that are permitted to go visit other programs if they get picked up. So transportation can be a tremendous blessing.

Music

Music is vital at a drug program. It creates an atmosphere and must be emphasized for its importance in recovery. Live music is ideal, but for starters you can use a CD player. Play relevant Christian worship music. If it is old time church hymns, sorry, it is going to turn the attendees off! Music is powerful in the world and we need to show we have relevant music as well. (Interesting note: A lot of attendees always seemed to be musicians. Eventually you can put them to work!)

Follow-Up

This is probably the most important part of any outreach yet, our work schedules can sometimes make it the hardest thing to do! If you're not able to be consistent to follow up on a weekly basis, find a volunteer who can. It is important that only men call men and women call women, too. Most people prefer being contacted by email anymore, but a phone call does make it more personal. It is said without follow up in the first 48 hours, you will lose the people, so you need to immediately reach out. And remember to limit your call to just a "welcome back" call and not a prayer or counseling session!

Record Keeping and Accountability

This is as important as follow-up. Most churches are required by law to keep confidentiality forms of all attendees on file. A church wants to do this anyway for liability purposes, because the recovery program is not a counseling program and to get that acknowledgement from the attendees is vital. Record keeping involves keeping up with the addresses and other pertinent information, as well as how many visits the attendee came for in case it is needed for the courts. Your church may require a weekly or monthly report, but an annual is a must!

Sponsors

We do not have sponsors. Other people in the program to hold one another accountable and call in time of need. But you can have workers who call and follow up on the attendees. Most churches have an emergency hotline that people can call in times of crisis. My thinking on sponsors is that two people in the same ditch can't help each other out. There must already be someone out who can pull the other to safety. And that person has long been in the recovery process; otherwise you will just be finding yourself another party buddy! This has happened way too many times! Only the strong can support the weak, as it says in Galatians 6. We have also learned it isn't good to always be calling someone every time there is a crisis, but to learn to rely on God and call out to Him through these difficult but temporal times. This is how we grow in the Lord and learn to ride out the storms of life.

ABOUT THE AUTHOR

Cynthia Major Almaraz

A product of the "hippie movement" of the 70's, 19- year-old Cynthia was ready for a change. She dropped out of school during 8th grade, ran away from home 13 times until she left for good, hooking up with a gang of misfits. She was so tired of running from the law, getting high day after day, and feeling like there was no future in sight for her and her 3 year old son. So she did what she did best, ran away!

Cynthia's life was radically changed after she bought a one way plane ticket to south Texas in 1977, leaving her home of Pittsburgh, Pennsylvania in search for a better life. She had hopes of turning over a "new leaf." However, it was all disrupted when she was caught up in a drug bust.

While incarcerated for over four months, she received Christ after reading some books that were circulating in the jail: I Believe in Visions by Kenneth E. Hagin and The Cross and the Switchblade (story of Nicky Cruz) by David Wilkerson. She had hope that she would be released and that all things would be restored, including her son, though authorities said because she's doing time, was an addict, and an unfit mother and she would never see her boy again.

Pastors B.B. and Velma Hankins and the West Columbia Christian Center frequented the jailhouse every Sunday afternoon. They became family upon her release. She said, "They showed me the love of Jesus by visiting me in jail. When I got out, they fed

332

me, clothed me, gave me a job, cared for my baby through loving members, and most of all, they mentored me. The church even raised money to send me off to Bible College. And I always had a place to call home during the summers and holidays. I felt like I was someone important to them and didn't want to let them down. They believed in me, therefore, I was able to believe in myself!"

Cynthia has never returned back to the former lifestyle of addictions. She attributes this milestone to the Word of God and His love shown through His people. "He found me and He saved me from my destructions," she says.

In 1980, she obtained an Associates Degree in Theology from Christ for the Nations Institute, Dallas, Texas. Cynthia also graduated from Rhema Bible Training Center of Broken Arrow, OK, in 1981 and then again in 2006. She also attended The School of the Local Church in 1998 under the leadership of Bob Yandian (a student of Charles Duncomb). She attributes in-depth knowledge of the Word of God to all the years of Bible training and over 20 years of serving under the influence of Pastor Yandian.

Cynthia has pressed on to achieve more accomplishments in her life. One was being fully pardoned by then Governor George W. Bush in 1996. After that, she was able to obtain her Bachelors in Education. Then for over a decade as an intervention teacher, she helped young people dare to believe in a better life by not giving up on their dreams. Finally, in 2013, Cynthia obtained her Masters in Administration from Oral Roberts University.

She is married to Robert J. Almaraz. Together they have five children and three grandchildren. Cynthia is also, an ordained minister. Milestones was first written in 2008. Her second book, an autobiography enttitled A Girl called Sin, should be released in the summer of 2015.

Cynthia Major Almaraz has been a guest speaker several times on the Trinity Broadcasting Network, sharing her testimony of hope and deliverance. Her husband Robert is a powerful Bible teacher who preaches the love of Christ and the importance of allowing healing to take place in the soul through the Word of God. Together they make a dynamic team for Christ, teaching and preaching to the hurting and the addicted in the Body of Christ! "Yes, addictions do come to church," she says, "and what better place to help them in the house of God where we have been helped!" After all, Jesus said in Matthew 11:28, "Come to me, all you who are weary and heavy burdened and I will give you rest."

PRAYER OF SALVATION

God loves you—no matter who you are, no matter what your past. God loves you so much that He gave His one and only begotten Son for you. The Bible tells us that "...whoever believes in Him shall not perish but have eternal life" (John 3:16 NIV). Jesus laid down His life and rose again so that we could spend eternity with Him in heaven and experience His absolute best on earth. If you would like to receive Jesus into your life, say the following prayer out loud and mean it from your heart.

Heavenly Father, I come to You admitting that I am a sinner. Right now, I choose to turn away from sin, and I ask You to cleanse me of all unrighteousness. I believe that Your Son, Jesus, died on the cross to take away my sins. I also believe that He rose again from the dead so that I might be forgiven of my sins and made righteous through faith in Him. I call upon the name of Jesus Christ to be the Savior and Lord of my life. Jesus, I choose to follow You and ask that You fill me with the power of the Holy Spirit. I declare that right now I am a child of God. I am free from sin and full of the righteousness of God. I am saved in Jesus' name. Amen.

If you prayed this prayer to receive Jesus Christ as your Savior for the first time, please contact us on the Web at **www.harrisonhouse.com** to receive a free book.

Or you may write to us at

Harrison House • P.O. Box 35035 • Tulsa, Oklahoma 74153

The Harrison House Vision

Proclaiming the truth and the power

Of the Gospel of Jesus Christ

With excellence;

Challenging Christians to

Live victoriously,

Grow spiritually,

Know God intimately.